MEMORABLE DAYS

Books by James Salter

The Hunters (1957)
The Arm of Flesh (1961)
A Sport and a Pastime (1967)
Light Years (1975)
Solo Faces (1979)
Dusk and Other Stories (1988)
Burning the Days (1997)
Cassada (2000) (rewritten version of *The Arm of Flesh*)
Gods of Tin (2004)
Last Night (2005)
There & Then (2005)
Life is Meals (2006)

Books by Robert Phelps

Heroes and Orators (1958)
Letters of James Agee to Father Flye (1962)
Twentieth-Century Culture: The Breaking Up (1965)
Earthly Paradise (1966)
The Literary Life (1968)
Professional Secrets (1970)
Belles Saisons: A Colette Scrapbook (1978)
Letters from Colette (1980)
The Collected Stories of Colette (1983)
Colette: Flowers and Fruit (1986)
Continual Lessons (1990)

JAMES SALTER

ROBERT PHELPS

MEMORABLE DAYS

The Selected Letters of James Salter and Robert Phelps

Edited by John McIntyre

Foreword by Michael Dirda

COUNTERPOINT
BERKELEY

Library of Congress Cataloging-in-Publication Data
Salter, James.
Memorable days : the selected letters of James Salter and Robert Phelps / by James Salter and Robert Phelps ; edited by John McIntyre; foreword by Michael Dirda.
p. cm.
ISBN-13: 978-1-58243-605-0
ISBN-10: 1-58243-605-3
1. Salter, James—Correspondence. 2. Phelps, Robert, 1922—Correspondence. I. Phelps, Robert, 1922- II. McIntyre, John, 1978- III. Title.
PS3569.A4622Z48 2010
813'.54—dc22
[B]
2010005453

Frontispiece: James Salter, courtesy of author; Robert Phelps, courtesy of Peter Deane.

Interior design by David Bullen

Printed in the United States of America

COUNTERPOINT
1919 Fifth Street
Berkeley, CA 94710

www.counterpointpress.com

Distributed by Publishers Group West

10 9 8 7 6 5 4 3 2 1

Contents

. . . .

Foreword

By Michael Dirda

As one reads through the correspondence between Robert Phelps and James Salter, it gradually becomes clear that these are love letters. The talk is of the literary life, of magazine pieces, plays and movies, of revered "makers" like Colette and Stravinsky, of long walks in Greenwich Village and loneliness in Aspen, Colorado. But quite plainly the two writers—both married, both moving in glamorous circles—cannot get enough of each other. Six months after they first meet, Salter writes from Colorado: "Why don't you work here? I miss you and there's nobody to speak *avec*."

Nearly anyone who ever spent an afternoon or evening with Robert Phelps will attest to his wondrous charm. Composer Ned Rorem, writers Dan Wakefield and Stephen Koch, poet Richard Howard—all these have memorialized Robert's perennial youthfulness, his generosity of heart and spirit, his genius for friendship. At a recent panel on "New York in the 1950s," sponsored by the Associated Writing Programs, Phelps was named the very embodiment of that era's literary life.

He and I first met in May of 1968, when I was nineteen years old. I was on my way to a summer in France and en route stopped in New York, my very first visit to the city. Somehow I managed to figure out the subways and eventually emerged at Union Square, then strolled, wide-eyed, through bright sunshine to 6 East 12th Street. After I'd rung the buzzer on the mailbox, Robert came bounding down the stairwell, two steps at a time. He was the father of my college roommate but might have been his brother: black tousled hair, white T-shirt, corduroy jeans, Clark Wallabees on his feet and a boyish grin on his face. We trudged up the steps to his book-lined eyrie on the fourth floor, and by the end of that afternoon—of literary gossip, accompanied by two robust Tanqueray martinis—I was drunk. I also knew that I wanted more than anything in life to be him.

We came from similar backgrounds. I grew up in Lorain, Ohio, eight miles from his hometown of Elyria; I was attending Oberlin College, where he'd spent a year or so. Most of all, though, I too had long dreamed about being a writer in New York, of living by my pen and wits in an apartment full of books—real, hardcover books. On that first day, Robert showed me a set of uncorrected page proofs of Randall Jarrell's *The Third Book of Criticism*, which he'd been assigned to review. I'd never seen page proofs before. Little did I know that I was looking at my own future.

At that time Robert and his wife, the painter Rosemarie Beck, shared a large two-room apartment with kitchen and bathroom. But Robert actually worked in a little cubby off the brownstone's stairwell on the second floor, a kind of janitor's closet fitted out with a desk and a chair and a few shelves. Its window looked out on 12th Street, and sometimes passersby could glimpse the writer or his shadow typing away. Only later were Robert and Becki able to rent another floor in their building so that he was finally able to furnish a room of his own.

Naturally, Robert transformed this new space into what Auden once called "a cave of making." The wooden floors were stained black, the walls completely lined with bookshelves. Curtains, usually kept drawn, blocked out both day and night. A pole lamp stood next to a rather high-tech chrome and leather easy chair, and extension lights were clamped to the corners of bookcases. On a coffee table in the middle of the room there always lay page proofs, literary magazines, publishers' catalogues. Instead of a sofa, a daybed butted up against the back of a freestanding bookcase and was covered with pillows embroidered with scenes from classical mythology (Becki's handiwork). They were like small Poussins in needlepoint. Near the music corner—lots of Stravinsky, Poulenc, and Ravel LPs—stood a long, low set of white shelves, on top of which rested more books, some heavy tumblers, and a big bottle of Tanqueray gin.

The books in Robert's library were read again and again, underlined and marked up, made very much his own. Since he preferred the muted tonal-ities of book cloth, few had kept their bright and garish dust jackets. But before discarding the djs, Robert would sometimes cut out the author photos and glue them into an oblong album labeled "The Poet's Face." Amplified with chronologies, lists and anecdotes, this eventually became his lover's homage to writers and writing, *The Literary Life: A Scrapbook Almanac of the Anglo-American Literary Scene from 1900 to 1950* (coauthored with his friend Peter Deane).

So it was that in this comfortable living room–bedroom–study, Robert padded about, surrounded by his favorite authors, most of whose works he owned, in toto: W. H. Auden, Colette, Cyril Connolly, Glenway Wescott, Louise Bogan, Jean Cocteau, Marcel Jouhandeau, James Agee, Pier Paolo Pasolini, Rayner Heppenstall, Paul Léautaud, Brigid Brophy. Pick out one of their well-worn books from the shelves, and you might find inside an old postcard from the author; or a quotation copied onto the endpapers (*"Art is concerned with production" —Aristotle*, appropriately in a bibliography of Henry James); or a review clipped from a newspaper; or even, in the case of T. S. Eliot, a commemorative postage stamp. In his copy of Robert Lowell's *Lord Weary's Castle*, Phelps noted that in 1946 he had stolen the book from a department store in Cleveland. A first edition, too. When Robert Phelps loved a book, it became his book, as much as the author's.

Robert's work desk was simplicity itself: a sheet of painted plywood across two low metal filing cabinets. Near at hand, reference works: a Larousse French dictionary, the *Concise Oxford English Dictionary*, the little *Annals of English Literature 1475–1950* ("the principal publications of each year together with an alphabetical index of authors with their works"). Robert craved facts, dates, and odd particularities and once expounded a theory about Shakespeare's love life, based on a careful study of the birthdays and stage productions listed in Charles Williams's concise version of E. K. Chambers's biography. He speculated, with a Jesuitical logic that Stephen Dedalus would have envied, that the bard's brother must have cuckolded him. As I recall, on that same afternoon, he mock-solemnly intoned that a critic really only needed to know three things about writers: their sexual tastes, the state of their health, and where or how they got their money.

On the wall above the plank work table hung a four-by-six-foot bulletin board adorned with notes, pictures, more quotations, and even hand-cast astrological charts. In the center Robert had pinned a photograph of himself strolling down a country road in tennis shoes with novelist Glenway Wescott; next to it an exhortation from Auden: "We were put on earth to make things." In those days, Robert always typed on a portable manual typewriter, preferring to use yellow, green, blue, or even pink paper. It was like a Christmas treat to receive a letter from him and discover inside splashes of color, cool aquamarine, soft goldenrod. He thus brightened not only the day but many days, for his letters would be read and reread, like this one from MacDowell Colony, written to me in the early 1970s. I quote only one paragraph of many:

> I'm working on a memoir-novel this month, with a quiet cabin deep, deep in the birch and maple woods. I have a piano to bang on when I'm blocked and I croak Schumann and Poulenc to my own accompaniment. I'm here from 8:15 to four. Then I go back to my sleeping room, shave, nap, and at precisely 5:30 mix myself a massive Tanqueray martini (6 parts gin, 0.1 part very dry vermouth and a twist of lemon peel over four cubes of ice). Dinner's at 6:30 and by 8:30 I'm in bed with my Garzanti dictionary or Valéry or Renard. The autumn colors are the most beautiful I've ever seen in 15 years. Yesterday I drove 6 miles to visit Willa Cather's grave in a tiny village called Jaffrey Center . . . I think I have a review in next week's *Life*, or the one after that. At least I wrote it and they paid me; of Forster's posthumous novel *Maurice*.

Robert liked to quote the religious thinker Simone Weil—"We really possess nothing on this earth but the power to say I"—and he himself loved anything that revealed the personal, inner life of a creator, that made the writer present on the page as a breathing, human, preferably all-too-human being:

"Parable, fable, fiction," he once wrote, "are all fine. I want them. But whether I gracefully justify it or not, I also want diaries, letters, marginalia, table-talk, all the non-official forms by which men have also revealed their mystery, disguises, wishes, feints . . . Whenever a writer, any writer, uses some semblance of his own first person and tells me something about himself or the world around him which only he could have known, then a viable community of two is formed as I read. It can be a friend or a stranger. But more than the literary art is involved, and I must bring more than my safe aesthetic responses. The encounter may be joyous. It may also be maculate, messy, perturbing, as human relations often are."

In Robert's view, as he once confessed in a piece about Colette, "there are two classes of writers: those whose subject is the human heart, and those whose emphasis is upon all the other, perhaps more important possibilities in human experience. The latter include many of our most illustrious and bewitching contemporaries, from Valéry to Kafka, to Pirandello and Virginia Woolf. The former include all of my favorite writers, from Shakespeare to Jane Austen to Colette. Compare *All's Well that Ends Well*, *Persuasion* and *Julie de Corneilhan*. Does any writer know any more about love than the other? Aren't they in this respect peers, all three of them, for all the ages?"

Robert would certainly include James Salter in his first, preferred category. Writing to Salter on October 2, 1970, he says, "you are a minority of one; a new herb in the cabinet; and, at the least, the most romantic writer we have." Perhaps the most erotic and heartbreaking, too. When Robert later inscribed a copy of Salter's *A Sport and a Pastime* for me, he called it "a book I love and envy." I was by then a graduate student in comparative literature at Cornell, with little time for unrequired reading, but I immediately sat down with the novel and finished it in one evening. Related in sentences as clear as rainwater, this story of a love affair between a young American and a French girl was a paean to the life of the senses and to driving cars and sex and France itself. Its final paragraph is perfectly simple and—given all that has gone before—utterly heartrending:

"As for Anne-Marie, she lives in Troyes now, or did. She is married. I suppose there are children. They walk together on Sundays, the sunlight falling upon them. They visit friends, talk, go home in the evening, deep in the life we all agree is so greatly to be desired."

Soon afterward, on trips to New York and Boston, I began to prowl used bookshops for Salter's two earlier novels, *The Hunters*, about Korean fighter pilots, and *The Arm of Flesh* (now called *Cassada*). Was it at Dauber and Pine or Biblo and Tannen that I unearthed a copy of *The Paris Review* with his appreciation of the Italian writer (and pilot) D'Annunzio, an essay arranged as a kind of alphabet of anecdotes? I even searched through back issues of *People* magazine so that I might read Salter's profiles of Nabokov and Graham Greene. Robert used to say—quoting Auden, I think—that the true test of one's devotion to an author was the willingness to collect his or her occasional journalism. In Salter's case, I was more than willing, I was eager for everything from his pen.

In 1975 *Light Years* appeared—Salter's achingly beautiful account of family life, marriage, and divorce, the *Tender Is the Night* of our time: "Life is weather. Life is meals. Lunches on a blue-checked cloth on which salt has spilled. The smell of tobacco. Brie, yellow apples, wood-handled knives." Just before publication, *People* loyally ran a brief, gossipy article about the author, accompanied by a small picture of Salter dressed in a cream-colored suit. With his mustache and dashing good looks, he might have been a 1930s film star. I bought that issue at the newsstand.

By the time *Solo Faces* appeared a few years later, in 1979, I was a young staff writer and editor for *The Washington Post Book World*. In the course of my review of that still underappreciated novel, I wrote that the great theme of Salter's fiction was "spiritual integrity," the pure and the impure. Ascents and descents—both real and symbolic—govern the action of *Solo Faces*, for its protagonist, Vernon Rand, is depicted as a kind of anchorite alpinist, whose heroic sanctity and simplicity as a climber is gradually undermined by publicity, women, this fallen world.

In particular, I tried to characterize Salter's unobtrusively seductive style, speaking of its "lyric gravity" and the exactness of his diction, pointing to his "precisely rendered surfaces," his avoidance of psychologizing, the prose music in his carefully pitched and weighted sentence fragments. I noted, too, how economically he reused details, imbuing a casual observation with metaphorical richness. For instance, early on Rand is described as wearing what look to be "the clothes of two or three vanished companions" and as resembling "some kind of holy man." Later in Paris, as he is growing sleek and soft, his sexual attractiveness is said to derive from his "ability to look good in old clothes." Thus, concluded *The Washington Post*'s earnest young reviewer, even the trappings of the spiritual may be demeaned and corrupted. Rand's downfall finally comes when he fails to live up to his own principles. "On his first climb in France, Rand tells a fellow climber, 'Never trust a piton you don't put in yourself.' But on his last climb he ties off on a piton already in the face."

In closing the review, I suggested that this "beautifully composed" book would remind readers of Camus and Saint-Exupéry, adding—quite correctly—that "It exemplifies the purity it describes."

Shortly after the piece appeared, Salter himself unexpectedly phoned up—he was in Washington, might he drop by—and we were soon sipping coffee in the *Post* cafeteria and talking about writing and Colette and Isaac Babel and, of course, Robert Phelps.

By then our friend's shaky paw had been diagnosed as Parkinson's disease, and writing had become extremely difficult for him. Still, with what effort I can't imagine, about this time he produced a superb review for Book World—a front-page review—of an early biography of Auden by Charles Osborne. Unable to work much on his own writing, Robert instead focused his energies on his teaching. Whether at Manhattanville College or the New School, his classes would always end up discussing his favorite works of prose or poetry—and these could be distinctly original, *echt* Robert: D. H. Lawrence's memoir of Maurice Magnus, the libretto of *The Magic Flute*, Colette's short story "Bella-Vista," short novels like Henry Green's *Loving*, Glenway Wescott's *The Pilgrim Hawk*, James Agee's *Let Us Now Praise Famous Men*, and Cyril Connolly's *The Unquiet Grave*. Robert once wrote to me about these classes:

> The kids are square and semi-literate but not unvaliant. Most of them stay awake at least. To my surprise they liked Cavafy, including his erotic side which, of course, I emphasized. Auden they respected but were bored by—too many big words. Firbank was too campy-seeming for them to take "seriously," but they loved Forster's *Where Angels Fear to Tread*. Next week, Genet, whom most of the class regard as a gay-lib Terry Southern. I must disabuse them.

Through some magic Robert could make any piece of writing subtly his own, even a classroom syllabus. One course, entitled "Available Light," is headed with two lines from Wallace Stevens: "After all, they knew that to be real each had / To find for himself, his earth, his sky, his sea." It ended with a sentence from Christopher Smart's "Jubilate Agno": "For I have seen the White Raven and Thomas Hall of Willingham and am myself a greater curiosity than both." In Robert's classes there were never any final exams. As he used to say, once again citing his beloved Auden, "Thou shalt not answer questionnaires / Or quizzes upon World Affairs / Nor with compliance / Take any test . . . "

Throughout his life, and especially in his later, illness-plagued years, Robert was tormented by a sense of failure, of never having fulfilled his promise. Yet his work has lasted. In his annotations to *Memorable Days*, editor John McIntyre refers to the neglected novel *Heroes and Orators*, as well as the essential books on Colette, especially the biographical *Belles Saisons* and the anthology *Earthly Paradise*. (In his memoir *Burning the Days*, Salter writes that the latter was "the favorite book of my daughter and was buried with her.") But Phelps also edited the letters of James Agee to Father Flye, Ned Rorem's early diaries (which he encouraged the composer to publish), Louise Bogan's essays on poetry, the autobiographical writings of Jean Cocteau (*Professional Secrets*), and the journals of Glenway Wescott. I can vouch that there are few better browsing books than *The Literary Life*, a "calendar view of literature in England and America" during the first half of the twentieth century, comprising "pictures, gossip, homage, warnings, and clues—together with laurels, letters, lists, and whispered asides." As it happens, this oversized album was published in 1968, and, with typical generosity, Robert sent me a copy that September, not long after we had first met. I've carried *The Literary Life* around with me ever since; it has been on my bedside table wherever I have lived. In one of his letters, Salter refers to it as his favorite book in the world.

Jim—as I will now call him—phoned on several of his subsequent visits to Washington. Once, when he was staying at the Tabard Inn, we arranged to have dinner together. I remember seeing him standing outside the hotel's front door: a well-cut brown sport jacket and slacks, the erect carriage, his handsome features. As we later sipped a drink while waiting for our table, he casually bantered with the female bar tender. To an envious me, Jim exemplified that most attractive of the fairy gifts, what the Italians call *sprezzatura*, an easygoing nonchalance, an innate gracefulness. He moved fluidly, like an outdoorsman or the ex-military man he was. When he spoke, his tenor voice was soft, his words measured, the thought precisely formulated. Lines actually wrinkled at the corners of his eyes when he smiled or joked. No wonder that James Salter has always been irresistible to women—while remaining a guy's guy too. When he stood up to receive the PEN/Faulkner Award for *Dusk and Other Stories*, the front row of the auditorium was lined with generals, former West Point classmates and Air Force buddies.

Jim and Robert corresponded frequently, if sometimes irregularly, with each other until the latter's death from cancer in 1989. Either one of them could dash off the kind of letter that would take most of us a week to compose. Yet *Memorable Days* isn't only a marvelous double portrait of two working writers, it's also a primer on life *tout court*. Here's Salter admonishing Phelps (and himself): "We must catch the train, Robert, we must move, otherwise life takes you, makes you soggy. We're wearing cheap shoes, we must stay ahead of it." And here's part of a long letter from Phelps to Salter. It deserves to be quoted at length:

> Your letters are part of my gospel. It seems to me it was only Monday morning that I read your Rome letter as I walked across Union Square (and under the equestrian statue of Geo. Washington which Henry James described in *An International Episode*) on my way to cover an overdraft at the bank . . . And now, Friday morning, again on my way to the bank, I find you're back in Aspen.
>
> You are wrong about my "life." It would be correct only if it were productive of worthy books. As it is, for 20 years, I have only scrounged at making a living: a low standard of survival and hundreds of articles, reviews, flower arrangements of other people's prose, etc. Not a good form of hell at all. This has become terribly clear to me in the past 6 weeks when I have been going through sheaves of old printed matter with a view to making our publisher a book called *Following*. I have been appalled by the waste, the thousands and thousands of irretrievable words on which nevertheless I worked long and hard and sometimes until 5 A.M. No. Somewhere I took a wrong turning. I should not have tried to earn my living with my typewriter. I should have become a surveyor, or an airline ticket salesman, or a cat burglar. As it is, I am far far beyond the point of no return and such powers as I once counted on—the ability to write to order and out of my own battiness, so to speak—are suddenly gone. All this week I have tried to write two thousand words on *Don Quixote* for *Playbill* (sic). The pay is honest: $300. The assignment would have thrilled me ten years, five years ago. But today I am sterile, mute, empty-headed, helplessly, obstinately uninspired. Even Dexedrine is no help. And at times my poor right hand shakes so violently I have to laugh. The message is explicit: no more hacking, which is to say, no more earning a living at this "desk of a man who cannot be bought," etc.

> Thank God I have a teaching assignment next semester. That may be a temporary solution. Meantime I fret and read and walk around Manhattan. Do you know about Ravel? In his last five years, he suffered from a brain tumor which gradually paralyzed his mind. One day his great friend Hélène Jourdan-Morhange visited him and found him sitting on his balcony at Montfort-L'Amaury. "What are you doing?" she asked, and Ravel looked down at her and replied, "*J'attends.*" . . .
>
> Meantime we have had a glorious nor'easter, which came smashing through one of my front windows, hurtling broken glass and manic water all over me as I lay in bed. And I have dined with Miss Lucia Marinetti—daughter of the futurist—elegant but too Milanese (business-minded) per me; and helped celebrate John Cage's 60th birthday, or birth-year; and listened to the election returns (but only until 10:30), after which I went back to my book-of-the-month, Quentin Bell's biography of his aunt Virginia Woolf. Superlative. Don't believe that dreary square on the front page of *The NY Times*.
>
> Today our Jamaican maid Rosa is here, singing to herself, murmuring to the cat, and generally swabbing about. For lunch she only wants a pint of Häagen-Dazs ice cream—carob flavor, preferably. It's lovely here today—shiny-bright air, Viking blue sky, fire engines shrieking on Fifth Avenue, a letter from Aspen in the mailbox.

After Robert's death, Jim and I continued to meet from time to time. At a restaurant near Washington's Union Station, he introduced me to his wife, Kay, and the talk that afternoon ranged from our sons to recent books to life in the Hamptons. One evening, at a publication party given by publisher Jack Shoemaker, we chatted about the moving portrait of Robert in *Burning the Days*: "It was not for his wisdom I was drawn to him, rather for his presence, which confirmed all I sought to feel about the world . . . He was one of the most important influences in my life and in whatever I wrote afterwards. Would this interest him, I often wondered? Would he find it deserving?" And once

Jim and I actually ran into each other in Paris. I was there to be part of a UNESCO panel on the future of American fiction, and there was a concurrent festival celebrating contemporary American writers. A number of distinguished novelists had been invited.

That evening, under gigantic *Arabian Nights*–style tents, French fans listened to the visiting writers discourse or crowded round them for autographs. While Jim and Kay asked me to come to dinner after his book signing, I was obliged to go off to an official cocktail party of some sort. So we only had a few minutes together. But, as from the first, as always, we soon started to speak about Robert, while all about us people were sipping white wine, pretty girls and boys were flirting, classical music played in the background, and everywhere the talk was of books and writing and *le roman américain*. Certainly, the literary life can seldom have looked so alluring. He should have been here, we said.

Michael Dirda is a Pulitzer Prize–winning critic and the author of the memoir An Open Book *and of four collections of essays:* Readings, Bound to Please, Book by Book, *and* Classics for Pleasure.

. . . .

Introduction

By John McIntyre

> At the very end of 1969, *A Sport and a Pastime* having been published with sales of a few thousand copies, I received a fan letter, long, intelligent, and admiring . . . James Salter, *Burning the Days*

The letter was from Robert Phelps, a writer who had published one novel, hundreds of book reviews, and a number of singular books of bricolage that employed the knowledge and insight of a biographer. Composer and author Ned Rorem has characterized Phelps as a "frantic Francophile"; naturally, *A Sport and a Pastime* won Phelps's admiration, for it is a novel that follows a love affair between a young American man and a French shopgirl in "green, bourgeois France." But it was not until the release of *Three*, a 1969 film Salter directed, starring Charlotte Rampling and Sam Waterston, that Phelps actually initiated their correspondence.

Salter was born James Horowitz in 1925 in Passaic, New Jersey. He grew up in New York City and planned to attend Stanford before receiving a last-minute appointment to West Point. Though he was unprepared for military life—he describes himself then as "seventeen, vain, and spoiled by poems"—Salter persevered and entered the U.S. Army Air Force at the end of his tenure as a cadet in 1945. World War II ended before he could see action. An accident in training delayed his entry into fighters, but he had atoned for this early miscue by the time the Korean War started. He flew a hundred-plus missions during the war, recording one kill and damaging another enemy plane.

Salter resigned his commission in 1957, following the publication of his first novel, *The Hunters*, which dealt with the life of a fighter pilot during the Korean War. Considerable risk was involved in moving from military to civilian life, a fact he acknowledges in *Burning the Days*; on the day he resigned, he recalls, "as I walked into the Pentagon I felt I was walking to my death."

He remained available as a reserve for several years afterward and returned to active duty for the Berlin Crisis in 1961, but as he says in *Burning the Days*, "That year, I understood, was the close of things." *The Arm of Flesh* was published the same year. Salter was able to write the book thanks to money earned from the sale of the film rights to *The Hunters*. This second novel, however, is a book Salter has since expressed dissatisfaction with, to the extent that he made heavy revisions to it before allowing it to be rereleased as *Cassada* in 2000.

It was his next work, *A Sport and a Pastime*, published in 1967, which established Salter as a *sui generis* prose stylist, and two years later, after writing *Downhill Racer*, a film which starred Robert Redford, and directing *Three*, he met Robert Phelps. Salter was never again so involved in the film industry, though he did continue to write for the movies for some time afterward.

In fact he was still writing them when he began work on his next novel, *Light Years* (1975), which is concerned with the dissolution of a marriage. Prior to the book's publication, Salter met Kay Eldredge, who later became his second wife. Though he was divorced the same year *Light Years* was published, Salter has made it clear on a number of occasions that Nedra and Viri, the couple in the book, are not modeled on him and his first wife.

His connection to Robert Redford and the urging of the legendary mountain climber Bob Craig led Salter to research and write a climbing-themed script in the aftermath of *Light Years*. The film was never made, but at the insistence of Robert Ginna, editor-in-chief at Little, Brown, Salter turned the script into his next novel, *Solo Faces* (1979).

During the 1980s, Salter turned to journalism, travel writing in particular, as an alternative to writing for the movies, an experience he had found frustrating. The decade also marked the appearance of his first book of short fiction, *Dusk and Other Stories*. The collection was well received, earning the PEN/Faulkner Award in 1989.

Though he had long been reluctant to do so, in 1997 Salter published a book about his own life, *Burning the Days*, again due to the interest of an editor, this time Joe Fox at Random House. The book is not a traditional memoir. Instead Salter has said, it "was reminiscence and it spoke about things during certain periods of time in my life as well as I can tell the truth about them."

Salter was unsatisfied with his second novel, *The Arm of Flesh*. He rewrote the book and it was reissued in 2000 as *Cassada*. A book culled from his Korean War-era journals, as well as selections from his other writings about flying, appeared in 2004. A second collection of short fiction, *Last Night*, was published to wide acclaim in 2005. Since then, a book of Salter's travel writing, *There and Then*, has been released, as well as *Life is Meals: A Food Lover's Book of Days*, a lovingly produced volume he co-authored with his wife, Kay.

Robert Phelps was born in 1922 in Elyria, Ohio. He moved east in the 1950s and married the painter Rosemarie Beck, who lived in upstate New York. During those years, Phelps was a fixture at artists' colonies, in particular Yaddo and the MacDowell colony. These experiences fed his first and only novel, *Heroes and Orators*, which was published in 1958.

Two years later, he moved to Manhattan, resolving to make his living by his typewriter, as he put it. It was certainly a gamble, one which would succeed or fail based on the scope of his talent. He helped found Grove Press but it was sold soon after to Barney Rosset. Meanwhile, Phelps reviewed books as a means to pay the bills. He sometimes wrote more than one review per week, publishing them under pseudonyms.

His next significant work was *Earthly Paradise* (1965), an "autobiography" of Colette, comprised of selections from her own writings. He compiled *Professional Secrets*, a book of Jean Cocteau's life, in the same manner five years later. Phelps could have used the same materials in the service of standard biographies, but he opted to let the writers tell their own stories, so to speak. Rorem has written that, in such books, Phelps's "elucidation was creation," but the reality is that Phelps's willingness to let these authors' works speak for them has consigned him to the margins. It is apparent he was aware of this, as in a September 1971 letter to Salter, he writes,

> This moment I am editing a pilot sampler of 150pp. out of Glenway [Wescott]'s diaries, letters, obiter scripta, etc. for 1955. It's to go to Roger Straus, who wants to commission me to prepare 4 volumes of Wescott journals. It's like playing with paper dolls—all scissors and paste, with several colors of ink. I do it three hours every afternoon, and the only bad part is the temporary illusion it gives of covering pages. Alas, they're someone else's and as so often, I'm just a bridesmaid.

Phelps was responsible for a number of unique volumes, but perhaps his most singular work, a scrapbook almanac entitled *The Literary Life*, which he coauthored with Peter Deane, was published in 1968. Michael Dirda speaks to its composition in his essay earlier in this volume, but it bears mentioning that its mix of trivia, gossip, and major literary events is a decided pleasure to read.

Other volumes followed, among them *Belles Saisons*, a lovingly prepared scrapbook of Colette's life, and her *Collected Stories*, which Phelps edited. The final years before his death in 1989 resulted in two volumes: one final book on Colette, *Flowers and Fruit*, and *Continual Lessons*, a book composed of selections from Glenway Wescott's journals, published shortly after Phelps's death.

This, then, is Phelps's first new, published work in nearly two decades. Its roots lie in a very old friendship, and an enthusiasm of his, as evidenced in his letter from December 27, 1970. "Scrapbooks, footnotes, almanacs, letters, diaries, questionnaires, marginalia, memos, alphabets . . . how I love them," he writes. One hopes he would be pleased to see his own letters to Salter in print.

A Sport and a Pastime had been published two years before Phelps initiated their correspondence. Salter was then building the reputation he still holds for composing "American sentences better than anybody writing today," to quote the novelist Richard Ford. By 1970, though, Salter was struggling with a movie script he was having trouble getting produced. It must have galled him to think he might have been writing fiction instead, but there was the consolation of good money for the film assignments.

The correspondence that follows is composed of selections from a twenty-year exchange of roughly two hundred letters, ending with Phelps's death in 1989, from colon cancer. Across the whole of the volume, a fuller picture of Salter as a writer emerges, as in late 1975 when he describes this (for him) highly appropriate arrangement: "I'm writing on the same table on which I eat. Wonderful, warm confusion. Bits of Stilton, stains of tea."

After reading *Heroes and Orators*, Salter wrote that, "Of course, this was a youthful book. You had not yet found the stream-bed that runs from within to the page . . . you were only beginning to understand how to focus the enormous forces, the knowledge, and the anti-knowledge, within you." Salter's own youthful books (*The Hunters* and *The Arm of Flesh*) were behind him by that time. *A Sport and a Pastime* clearly proceeded from Salter's own "stream-bed," and so did other things he wrote during the two decades of the correspondence, his novel *Light Years* in particular.

Salter's admiration of Phelps was genuine, but Phelps's outlook on his own life was decidedly different. In a letter from November 7, 1972, Salter writes, "Your life is the correct life." The poet Richard Howard reflects Phelps's feelings in this regard as well, in a poem published on the occasion of Phelps's death, "For Robert Phelps, Dead at Sixty-six":

> Masterpieces you called "strenuous,"
>
> and were satisfied—or so you asserted—
> with patching up Colette, endless
> apprenticeships to other men's disclosures,
> Jouhandeau, Wescott, Cocteau—not "works"
>
> but the launching-pad that sends the rocket up.

When he contacted Salter, more than a decade after publishing *Heroes and Orators*, Phelps was struggling to produce another novel. Like Salter, he was devoting much of his time to work for immediate pay, in his case writing book reviews and journalism. The writer Dan Wakefield remembers Phelps talking of his novels in progress, "speaking of them as fondly as if they were the names of lovers." It is puzzling that Phelps never finished any of them. In his landmark book, *Love and Death in the American Novel* (1960), the critic Leslie Fiedler calls Phelps "a serious new writer" and *Heroes and Orators* "a complex and troubling study of homosexuality." Despite the good notices, Phelps did not publish a word of fiction in the final three decades of his life. The question of why yields complex answers.

Phelps's novel did explore homosexuality—although glancingly. He thought of himself as bisexual, but he remained married to painter Rosemarie Beck for over forty years. Phelps was uncomfortable with the identity he would have been assigned if his successive books also had homosexual themes, especially if they were more explicit. It's unclear whether this was due to a fear that being labeled a gay novelist would limit him as a writer or whether he was simply uncomfortable with being seen as gay. Howard speaks to this as well:

I wonder if the delicacy
of your domesticities (that son unseen,
 that wife dedicated to her art)

made your love for men the mirror type
 of mine, you the critical voyeur,
resisting "production," I proliferating
 among nameless bodies.

In a 1965 journal entry, Phelps considered becoming the world's "first bisexual novelist," but in other instances he referred to himself as a monster and saw his life as divided. Perhaps most unfortunate, Phelps believed that a trembling of his hand (later diagnosed as Parkinson's disease) was the result of this ambivalence. In a 1972 letter to Salter, he wrote, "My hand continues to shake. It's all neurotic, I'm sure. *Il faut payer*—but in my case, it's mostly for sins of omission, I'm afraid."

Rorem has described Phelps's letters as "witty, lewd, sage, generous, gossipy, aggressively self-effacing, monstrously opinionated without bitchery, engrossed by the literary life in general while being always directed to a unique recipient, and generally weaving something extraordinary out of something ordinary." These particular letters are notable for the time in which they were written as well, in the sense that they represent a friendship between a married straight man and a married gay or bisexual man, at a time when attitudes toward homosexuality were not so open as they are today. Michael Dirda calls them love letters, and rightly so, though they are not freighted with sexual implication. "From the first moment I recognized him for what he was," Salter writes of Phelps in *Burning the Days*, though the two never discussed Phelps's decision to remain married, to live in a way that must at times have been stifling.

Phelps and Salter quickly formed a genuine bond, one that survived 20 years of professional and personal changes of fortune. These letters, like Salter's reflections on Phelps in *Burning the Days*, are testament to that bond, as well as a reminder that Phelps was a passionate literary man, prematurely forgotten by readers.

MEMORABLE DAYS . . . .

1969–1970

Like the Year of a First Love

In 1969 James Salter was perhaps still capable of ambition concerning the film business, but he was already without illusions. Three *was not a success at the box office; by the end of 1970, any aspirations of being an auteur were abandoned. This is not to color him a failure. He continued to make money writing films for years to come, and that, as his experiences and the experiences of other writers show us, is one of the most reliable measures of success for a screenwriter. Fortunately the year was not totally abandoned to film work. He worked on a play,* The Death Star, *as well as "The Cinema," which eventually appeared in* Dusk and Other Stories. *Phelps had by that time established himself as a skilled and reliable reviewer and journalist, though even then he was unhappy with the balance between these paid assignments and the little attention he managed to give his fiction. He might have found solace in the publication of* Professional Secrets, *his "autobiography" of Jean Cocteau, created by compiling passages from Cocteau's own work. But it is perhaps no exaggeration that the highlight of the year for either man was their meeting in January of 1970.*

1969

. . .

Maggie Paley was part of The Paris Review *staff during the 1960s. She has since written a novel,* Bad Manners. *She also emerges quite winningly in the oral history of George Plimpton's life,* George, Being George.

. . .

December 24, 1969
New York

Dear Mr. Salter,
I have had your Nyack address (from Geo. Plimpton's Maggie Paley) for well over a year now, and during all this time, I have been intending to write you about *A Sport and a Pastime*, which—let's say—is my own favorite American novel of the '60s. Then, a couple of weeks ago, I came out of *Downhill Racer* in a trance of enthusiasm (at the script, I mean) and burbled a letter as I dodged Third Ave. traffic, but found a bar and talked myself out before getting home to the typewriter. Now I've seen *Three*, and I must make you some sort of sign, however hasty and inadequate to my multiple occasions.

I don't know the Irwin Shaw story, but you certainly make it your own; in fact, at times I was able to imagine that I was actually seeing your adaptation of *A Sport*. I loved every moment of the film (including one which troubles me: Taylor declining to spend the night with Marty, which seems to me ambiguous and unconvincing in the light of Taylor's own personality, or his relation to either Bert or Marty—*mais passons*). I think the ending is exquisite, elegant, eloquent. So is the beginning. So are dozens of shots all the way through—and I don't merely mean the ravishing landscapes (including the best of Florence I've ever seen anywhere). Mr. James Salter is a very refined and knowing maker; for my money, the best on the movie market this year. Over the coming weekend, I hope to get back to the Kips Bay and see his film several more times—especially to savor the pace, which I loved as much as the images or the storytelling. As in *A Sport*, you have an extraordinary nervous system: relaxed but quick, leisurely but alert, lambent but keen.

I'm also astonished at your professionalism. Apart from *Racer*, I assume this is your first film. But you handle the medium, and what I imagine must be its bewildering mechanics, with wonderful ease. I don't know which I feel more strongly: respect or envy. The only writer I've ever known with comparable gifts and sensibility—[James] Agee—died before he had a chance to make a film of his own.

Of course another American can't talk about your work without mentioning the quality of your sensuous response to the good earthly life—food, clothing, flesh, cars, water, hotels. The wistful Puritan is probably the only soul who can be so romantic and precise at the same time when contemplating or partaking in the earthly paradise . . .

I have no idea where you are at present, here or abroad, but if you're ever in town, I'd like to buy you a drink and ply you with questions.

1970

January 2, 1970
Aspen

Dear Robert Phelps,

I'm a great admirer of your book of Colette [*Earthly Paradise*]. I've given many copies away. Everything about it is beautiful. I love to pick it up. I'm *out here* working for the winter. Don't know when I'll be in New York but I look forward very much to meeting you.

Three, unfortunately, has not been drawing audiences, anyway not big enough for it to keep playing and the end may come by the time this reaches you.

Your letter gave me great pleasure.

James Salter

. . .

They met for the first time in mid-January 1970, at El Quijote, the Spanish restaurant of the Chelsea Hotel. Phelps was waiting at the bar. The talk was immediately comfortable, and though Salter noted that Phelps was better read than he, it wasn't something Phelps flaunted but an intrinsic part of his conversation, of his life. Other dinners followed, at Phelps's apartment on 12th Street, and at restaurants in the neighborhood. A growing fondness is evident in the letters following that first meeting, a fondness that did not die, as suggested by Salter's remark in Burning the Days *that he has never passed the Chelsea "without remembering, in the manner of a love affair."*

The "Yvonne" Phelps refers to is the painter Yvonne Thomas, who was part of the New York group that so changed American and world art between the 1940s and 1960s. She was French, quite beautiful, and had lived something of a glamorous life; she counted a dance with the Prince of Wales (later King Edward VIII) among the memorable evenings of her life. Both Salter and Phelps knew her, Salter because she was one of the prominent figures in the early days of Aspen. Salter has lived in Aspen for part of each year for the past four decades. She owned a large property there, inherited from her husband, who died in a fire. Phelps knew her through his wife, Rosemarie Beck, who was part of the same influential group of artists. Pauline Kael was perhaps America's preeminent film critic during her twenty-plus years at The New Yorker. *Joe Morgenstern is also a film critic. He was awarded the Pulitzer Prize for Criticism in 2005. Today he writes for the* Wall Street Journal.

. . .

January 26
Aspen

Dear Robert,
Yvonne Thomas was at the house last night, we were talking of you. You know her husband died in a fire here last year. She's rebuilding the house but there's been a lot of difficulty and she thinks perhaps it's Leonard telling her she ought not to do it. Never having known him I didn't know what to say. She looks very well and seems to be going through that crisis of irresolution that precedes getting to work.

It's summer here. Bright sun and sixty degrees, I spend the day yawning. You were right about the airplane crash. All on board were killed. It was about two miles from my house. The first fatalities they've ever had flying passengers, my nerves are shot anyway. I surrender my life whenever I get on a plane, I'm sure you're saying; a flyer, how can that be? Believe me, it can.

The trip to New York was the best I've ever had. It began with that dinner in El Quijote (the lamb chops were better than the cod, but believe me, their gazpacho is excellent) and all sorts of things seemed to flow from that. Please do call Ellie Silverman about the screening this week. I am hoping your vibrations will strike Pauline Kael and Joe Morgenstern or one of them anyway. You are my alter ego. The thing is, it all went so quickly. I wanted to stay longer—the odor of grass in the Chelsea corridors. Also to have dinner at your house that night. Yvonne says she'll help me with some of the French in Mérrimée . . .

Robert, you've been so good. I feel I'm swarming in and taking too much of your time. Please forgive me. I'm writing to Huguette Faget about you.

. . .

William Klein is an American filmmaker and photographer. Among his notable works are the documentaries Muhammad Ali, the Greatest *(which Phelps refers to as* Cassius le Grand*), and* Grands Soirs & Petit Matins, *which is concerned with the 1968 Paris uprising.*

. . .

February 1
New York

Dear Jim,

A pro-tem report:

It's now just about set that I'll go to London on March 17th; to Paris March 29th; and come back April 9th. I can't stay away any longer because I'm committed to a New School workshop this semester and three successive classes is all I can justifiably skip. But what I am most eager to do is get to Zurich in October, with a week of the *vendange* in France in September . . .

I saw *Cassius le Grand*, and admired Klein's nimble getting around with the camera. Talk about "imaginary gardens with real toads." But the limits of working with documentary *matériaux* seem to me very grave. I yearn for the structural presence, the conception and architecture that only invention makes possible. Do I sound too theoretical? I only mean that while I love the delicious unexpectedness, the live, still quivering reality which K.'s technique puts salt on the tail of, I am continually unsatisfied by the results he can create when he limits himself to such substance. And then, too, Cassius himself—though undoubtedly beautiful in the flesh and magnetic in flashes—is a somewhat tedious (for me) subject. The close-ups of Malcolm X were marvelous; I wish the movie had been about him . . .

Shall I write to Madame (or Mlle?) Faget? *Quel âge a-t-elle*? I remember your talking about her, but there was also a lady in Rome with whom I have mixed her up. Both had ciceronal gifts, huh?

Give Yvonne a bearhug. Mr. Salter, too. He's displacing an enormous part of my daily thoughts, wonderings, questionings, etc.

Robert

Roger Straus was very impressed by your visit; in fact, it put the whole office in a flap, and assorted young ladies are still complaining that I didn't escort you around and present you in person!

February 8 or 9
Aspen

Dear Robert,

Your letters are very strong, even narcotic. Sundays have been the worst and the most exultant days of my life. You should really stop reading scripts and other perishables and concentrate on your own book. I am still dining, like a long lunch in the sunshine, upon *The Literary Life*, I don't want it to end. Please tell Roger Straus how much I appreciate his gift, not to mention yours (plural). Huguette Faget, did I tell you this? Was an actress, later a journalist, her father I think a banker, she is a close friend of Jean Lacouture, Barrault, Georges Wilson, many actors, publishers, writers; she has a daughter in her twenties, she herself is in her forties but radiant, beautiful teeth, hair, she dances, she has a life, also a 2CV. She is very modest, she will not talk readily of herself. Considers Chez Allard the finest restaurant in Paris. Goes often to the theatre, concerts. She lives alone. Her cat's name is Pilou. She, I regret to tell you this, loves bullfighting (it is this flaw which keeps her in perspective). I have written her, I will again with the date of your arrival. You can write or call or both.

In London I think you should see Andrew Sinclair. You know about him, don't you? He's very interesting, an historian, novelist and cineaste, also a publisher of immortal film scripts (*Grande Illusion*, [*The Battleship*] *Potemkin*, *Jules et Jim*, etc.). His wife is dazzling in her own right, a writer too, militantly left, visitor to Cuba, worshipper of Guevara . . .

Anchor Books, this is really marvelous, are taking *Downhill Racer* to publish in script form, probably with an introduction, I just had this news before the weekend. It had been submitted to them before our visit to Roger Straus and though I would have liked him to see it, still Anchor is a wonderful house or sub-house and I have hopes they will do an interesting job with it. Of course, they're all talking about "a new fiction form" and other stupidities, but as long as they are excited by it . . .

My children keep saying, don't go back there (NY)—the air is the equivalent of smoking two packs of cigarettes a day, to say nothing of smoke inhalation in certain rooms in the Chelsea. A director must, among other things, create an atmosphere in which people can work.

We are at a great watershed of history, it's the terror of this that is so distracting. Humor is the surest line of explanation, however—it can accomplish what the earnest, the tragic, the agonizing almost always misses. I think it was Thurber who said: We are living in a time of great turmoil, at least I am.

The sun is so hot today. To work.

. . .

Louise Bogan was an American poet and the poetry editor of The New Yorker *for thirty-eight years. Among other honors, she was the 1945 poet laureate to the Library of Congress. Janet Flanner was for many years a writer for* The New Yorker, *their Paris correspondent. She was also bisexual, which may further account for Phelps's interest in her. Brigid Brophy was a British writer, also bisexual. Bill Maxwell (William Maxwell) was a longtime fiction editor of* The New Yorker *as well as an accomplished fiction writer. Cyril Connolly was a British writer, the editor of* Horizon *and author of works such as* The Unquiet Grave *and* Enemies of Promise. *Marcel Jouhandeau was a French writer, apparently bisexual, or anyway a gay man who was married to women on two separate occasions. He was of great interest to Phelps, who hoped to bring more attention to his work in translation, particularly his journals, but ultimately proved unable to do so.*

. . .

February 20
New York

Dear James,
This past week has been parceled up, or broken down, into so many unrelated parts that I feel like Humpty Dumpty. Suddenly it's Friday and I sit here baffled, sulky and wanting a refund, a re-run, a recount. Did I tell you on the phone that my European junket is temporarily off? The decision came two weeks ago, when a dear friend of mine died, a poet named Louise Bogan; and as I sat in one of those grotesque little "sitting rooms" at the Campbell Funeral Home, with Bill Maxwell on one side and Louise's daughter on the other (she writes the copy for the Chiquita banana ads!), a Voice told me I'd better finish a book of my own toot-tweet! Then the same week my Rockefeller dough arrived, more dollars than I've ever had at once in my life before; and I decided that I didn't really need to spend the weekend in Sussex with Cyril Connolly, nor have a vegetarian lunch with Brigid Brophy, nor even dine on eels with Janet Flanner, nor accompany 82-year-old Marcel Jouhandeau on one of his regular Thursday visits to a male whorehouse near the place Pigalle.

I have your laundry, by the way. Do you want me to file it on my bookshelf under "S"?

. . .

Salter was going to Charleston, SC in connection with a film treatment he was writing, based on Friedrich Dürrenmatt's book Traps. *Cesare Pavese was one of the major Italian writers of the first half of the 20th century. Among his best known works are* The Devil in the Hills *and* The Moon and the Bonfires.

. . .

March 1
Aspen

Dear Robert,
Isn't it terrible how dry you can be? All week I've tried to write a story, I know everything about it, I can almost read it and yet I can't seem to write a single paragraph which interests me. It's like looking for something in the dark, there's such a huge amount of chance in writing. I was reading Cesare Pavese mostly to thaw myself out, to prove it was possible, to excite myself. I love his style. There cannot be more than a thousand words in his vocabulary, at least the one he uses in the book, and working with these simple materials, with his hands tied, so to speak, there's no room for trickery. His observation, his choice, his path, everything must be absolutely true, because everything shows. There are no cosmetics. He claims to have been influenced by Defoe. I want to read Jonathan Swift's *Letters to Stella*. Also William Gass' *I Have No Time*.

I'm going to Charleston, S.C., for a week about March 10 and passing through N.Y. on the way home . . . I'm anxious to be back at the Chelsea . . .

. . .

Phelps's reference to Roger Straus as "our" publisher was wishful thinking. He suggested that Straus publish Salter's work, but nothing came of the proposition. In 2006, however, Farrar, Straus, and Giroux published an edition of A Sport and a Pastime.

. . .

March 4
New York

Dear James,
I haven't been able to write anything for two months. Or rather, I write and write but it's "fiction." I don't believe what I'm saying . . . I can't seem to forget myself long enough to get something written. I am sure Mark Rothko's suicide began with this sort of *échec* . . .

You'll think I've made this up, but I've been reading Pavese all the past week, too—and for the precise same reasons you have had. He is one of the great elegiac poets. Pavese's temperament reminds me of my own more than any other writer I've ever encountered. I don't mean this immodestly. I simply recognize my own instincts in him. I wish I had a little of his talent. Did you know he translated *Moby-Dick*?

I liked one of Bill Gass' stories ("In the Heart of the Heart of the Country"), but some of his other stuff, including a pretentious novel he's writing now and which I had to listen to excerpts from last summer, put me off. He can be very exact and prehensile with a sentence. In his early forties, he left a wife and children to run off with a nubile student. They're in Italy this spring, or will be, or were to have been.

Did you read Roger Straus's attack on the Nat. Book Awards? Ballsy guy, our publisher!

. . .

Luchow's was a German restaurant on 14th Street in New York. It boasted artworks by luminaries such as Francisco Goya and remained in operation for one hundred years, before finally closing its doors after a 1982 fire.

. . .

April 10
Aspen

Robert, my,
A great, a day-long storm of snow here. I love bad weather. That was a wonderful night at Luchow's. Your stories pour over me; I am in a different world, one where I recognize myself. And the dinner *chez toi* as well. I read all the Field poems the next morning; I don't know if I really like them that much, perhaps one or two.

Aspen is dry, both atmospherically and otherwise. Yvonne is coming to dinner tonight, together with a failed painter named David Michael. I'm going to ask some questions, we have a Ouija board that all these women believe in utterly. Last night while I was out they asked it if

I would get money for my film. It said, yes. When? In three months (that's longer than I'd like to wait, but anyway it's encouraging). I've been reading books I sent to myself from Charleston, *The Waning of the Old South Civilization*, books on rice plantations and low-country architecture. The most interesting or useful thing I've come up with is the daughter of a confederate general, her first name was Buck. I like the name Goucher College. The Crater (terrible battle). Monday I am plunging into the treatment. It's wasted time, but not completely wasted. At the end is some money.

I am in a state of calm, even of serenity. I am without distractions, without amusements even. The town is empty. My pulse from New York will take two weeks to run down, perhaps a month. We spent an hour with young Mr. Bronfman [Edgar M.], large holder of MGM, now ousted, who is making films independently. His offices, of course, are in the Seagram Building. A white-coated waiter from the Four Seasons, oh, all right, the Brasserie, brought coffee in a manner one finds only in Europe. In the kitchen everyone is quarreling. The snow floods down,

Dear Robert,

J.

. . .

Monica Vitti was an actress who appeared in numerous films, among them L'Avventura, La Notte, *and* Le Notti Bianchi.

. . .

April 18
New York

Dear James,
This morning came a 3-page letter from Philip Guston—all about *A Sport and a Pastime*, which he loves. "It's a work I will re-read more & more . . . " We had dinner together last week and I gave him my extra copy, inscribed "from the author by way of Phelps." Excuse the gall. I'm helplessly proprietary about whatever I love. It's a wonder I haven't

told people Salter is one of my pseudonyms. We must go to Chinatown, the three of us. Philip is a robust gourmand, even a gourmet. I've known him since 1947. His new work is fantastic—Piero della Francesca–cum–Bud Fisher (*Mutt & Jeff*). He'll have a huge show here in October, then go to Russia and Israel (where he is a great cultural hero) and spend the winter in Rome.

I sit here trying to write exactly 650 words for *Life* about a show of 19th century American painting, furniture, etc. at the Met. There is a 1796 Salem chest of drawers which was recently found in an attic, with its nine drawers being used for ripening pears!

Over the weekend I almost died of food-poisoning, having gone with Colette's daughter and Susan Sontag and her Neapolitan girl friend Carlotta something (looks like a skinny Monica Vitti) to an abominable Chinese restaurant somewhere on the Upper West Side . . .

I'm still looking for a shack by the sea. Do you know an agent named Gloria Safier? She's a pal of Colette, and she's half-promised me the upstairs of a gardener's garage in East Hampton. I must have green grass for my cat, and a table for the typewriter, and some salt air.

Meantime I must also buy a pair of shoes for my son's wedding. That's May 28th. The next day I'm changing my name to Roberto di Colpo.

. . .

To Warsaw *was a film script Salter had written the previous year and was trying to advance. [Robert] Bob Ginna wrote and produced films during the late 1960s and early 1970s. Salter knew him both in this context and later as editor-in-chief at Little, Brown. He is also the author of* The Irish Way: A Walk Through Ireland's Past and Present, *in which he takes a walking tour of Ireland. Peter Matthiessen is an American writer, the recipient of two National Book Awards, one in Nonfiction for* The Snow Leopard *(1980) and one in Fiction for* Shadow Country *(2008). He is also one of the founders of* The Paris Review.

. . .

April 21
Aspen

Dear Robert,

Well, what else did Guston say? Painters are sometimes fantastic readers. I used to think they were my best friends (as if we had compatible signs). I don't know any anymore, except Yvonne, and I don't know her, she's as nervous as a sparrow. Don't starve me. I'm out here gnawing on old crusts and spending hours with this ex-theology student, this foremost dramatist, and I get weary of it . . .

The reviews of *Brotherly Love*, which is Bob Ginna's film, have just arrived. Disastrous. I don't think it's opened yet, it was supposed to open at the Paris last Wednesday but didn't. A real whipping, and even though he's uncomplaining, I'm sure he's feeling it. Also, it doesn't help *Warsaw*. How long have I been back here, almost two weeks. I'm scrambling around trying to arrange the summer just like you. I don't know anybody nice enough for you in East Hampton, but I do know Peter Matthiessen slightly, he's nearby. They go fishing out in the bay for flounders, he and Ginna. The time I went with them Matthiessen laid open his knuckle to a white I was sure was bone, on the outboard motor. If I don't make this film I'll probably write all summer which could be better but once you make up your mind it's so hard not to do something. I long to see Europe once more. I'm sending you my cleanest copy of *A Sport and a Pastime*, uninscribed, since I know you like to, if I did write in it I'd say, in return for the beautiful books you've given me, I make this simple, egomaniacal gesture. Yes, we must talk sometime.

. . .

Phelps refers to "the essay book" in this April 25 letter, because he planned to contribute an essay on Salter's novel, A Sport and a Pastime, *to a book on undiscovered masterpieces of literature. Zoe Caldwell is a highly regarded actress, particularly for her work on Broadway. She has won four Tony Awards for her work in productions as varied as* The

Prime of Miss Jean Brodie *and* Medea. *She was born in Australia but makes her home in the U.S. Laurette Taylor was an actress in stage and silent film productions, including two King Vidor films,* Peg o' My Heart *and* Happiness. Peg o' My Heart *was a reprise of her acclaimed stage turn in the role, which was written for her by the author J. Hartley Manners when the two were romantically involved. Dan Wakefield is an American writer. Among his notable works is the novel* Going all the Way *and a book of nonfiction,* New York in the 50s. *Knox Burger was an editor and later a literary agent. Phelps would likely have been out of place with Burger, whose clients included mystery writers such as Donald Westlake and Lawrence Block. He also published Kurt Vonnegut's first work of fiction, "Report on the Barnhouse Effect," as editor of* Collier's Magazine.

. . .

April 25
New York

Dear Jim,

This is Saturday so the PO is closed, which means I cannot get the *Three* photographs and text off to you until Monday. Meantime, by way of old crusts to gnaw on, I enclose (a) Philip Guston's letter about J. Salter and (b) a note from the man editing the essay book I'll try to write about you in (early morning syntax). I've spoken to Philip since and not only he, but his wife Musa, love the book. When the three of you are next in town, we'll all go to a non-art movie together.

Your own letters are so beautifully holographed that I'm ashamed to reply on this battered old tinker-toy. But my fist just isn't legible.

And my head aches. Last night, and the night before that, I was at rehearsals of a play adapted from *Earthly Paradise*. I love watching any professionals at work. This company is adorable and Zoe Caldwell is the most astonishing (stage) actress I have seen since I was at the U. of Chicago and beheld Laurette Taylor in the early stages of *The Glass Menagerie*. The Colette script is hardly a play—mostly lyrical glints, apostrophes to the audience, and *mots*. But Zoe's performance, or incarnation, is uncanny. There are also two cats, real ones, who slip about the stage as though they were really in a Burgundian garden in 1888. It's a tiny company, very valiant, gutsy, gifted, dear. The theatre is on East 3rd St., off Avenue B, so far away from the rest of the world that there will be chartered buses to take people north after the show. I hope it's a success.

I still haven't written some copy for *Life* that was due Wednesday. A friend of mine, Dan Wakefield, told me I should change agents, as he just did, and get a man called Knox Burger who would sell me to *McCall's* (for $10,000—he said) to do a piece about Salter en route to Warsaw. But that seemed unlikely—leaving my present agent, I mean. He's a good friend and I wouldn't know how to do it . . .

Brotherly Love has opened here, and the reviews were rough. But I haven't seen the picture itself yet. I gather Ginna did not direct it but produced it, right?

I'll send the script of *Three* along with the pictures. You must use a page for the proper manuscript or you'll baffle some poor literary exegete in 50 years.

You didn't tell me you had a story coming in *Paris Review*—no mention at all of any story, except one in progress. When can I see it?

Here the trees (if you can find one) are in bud. There are sudden thunderstorms. I'm reading the galley proof of the Cocteau "autobiography."

. . .

The American poet Edward Field has published widely and received awards ranging from the Prix de Rome to an Academy Award for his narration of the 1964 documentary To Be Alive! *His memoir,* The Man Who Would Marry Susan Sontag and Other Literary Portraits of the Bohemian Era, *and* After the Fall: Poems Old and New *have been published in recent years.*

. . .

April 30
En route to Warsaw

Dear Robert,
I love your letters. Philip Guston's aren't bad either, I return it herewith. I've finished my work for the moment; I'm speaking of work I have to do, a long film treatment, and mailed it off to New York. I expect, I hope, to be summoned to appear, perhaps in a week or so. In the meantime I'm reading *Choses Vues* [a collection of first-person pieces by Victor Hugo to which Phelps introduced Salter]. The print is very small and I'm only using one eye so it takes time. I'm not reading it; I'm translating it into English. I'm also reading a couple of other books trying to gather the last of the necessary material for a play, I don't suppose it will ever be produced but I want to do something that's interesting to read.

The story in *The Paris Review* (strange, I have the impression of telling you everything) is about—hello, Robert Phelps, hello, Edward Field—movies. As a matter of fact, it's called "The Cinema" and it's filled with imperfect people though not as imperfect as I'd like. It may be a little too romantic, finally, I don't know. More and more I want to write about people who cannot modify themselves to reality, whose life looks like no one else's, people who stain your life.

Today, again, driving snows here. I've had a fire burning all afternoon, I have the beautiful feeling of winters in Italy (I've never spent one). I'm drinking tea without sugar and planning to live twenty or thirty more years with everything falling away from me but my notebooks and work (in my family, teeth and hair are yours to the grave)...

. . .

Yaddo is an artists' colony in Saratoga Springs, NY. It has a history of over one hundred years, and hosted Salter, Phelps, and Phelps' wife Rosemarie Beck at various times, in addition to countless other distinguished writers, composers, and visual artists. Philip Guston was a notable painter and printmaker in the New York School, which included many of the Abstract expressionists. The American painter Arthur Cohen's work is in the permanent collections of the Dallas Museum of Art and the Whitney Museum of American Art.

. . .

May 6
New York

Dear James, O—
Please keep me posted as to your easterly schedule. I urge this because I don't want to find myself otherwise tied up while you're here, and the month of May is beginning to look complicated. Among other things, a wedding!—my son's, for God's sake! Why didn't he have the sense to elope? But no, his Baltimore *belle-mère* has prevailed, and unless my "It" manages to break an ankle between now and the 28th, I shall actually have to attend.

Meantime, next Monday, the 11th, I shall be driving Becki (and about 900 pounds of paint, brushes, stretchers, turpentine, violin, etc.) to Saratoga Springs, where she'll be at Yaddo until June 1st—that is, except for rushing back here on two successive Fridays to finish up her classes at Queens College (where she has been voted the maddest art teacher west of Spain). Then on Tuesday, the 12th, I hope to get out to Fire Island for an overnight inspection of possible rooms, shacks, empty barrels, for August. The prospect of spending the entire summer here in this slow-motion explosion called Manhattan horrifies me.

At the same time there is a novel to be written, and miscellaneous chaff on the side, to pay the rent. This Friday, I am to have lunch at the 4 Seasons with an editor—don't laugh—from *McCall's*. I remember my mother, back in Ohio in the thirties, used to subscribe to this rag. It consisted of dress patterns and culinary hints then, but it now appears to have had a change of image, or whatever Madison Avenue says. Kurt Vonnegut has just done a piece on Biafra, and the mightiest masturbator of us all, P. Roth, is writing something about Cambodia. I don't know what is expected of me, but I suspect it's another go at Colette, or French women's views of French-kissing. Becki has a teenage model (girl) who is a fierce promoter of something called the "Gay Liberation Front." They have a magazine (non-pornographic, in fact firmly didactic, all about how the police and the Mafia work together to bully the 3rd, 4th, & 5th genders), meetings, manifestos, rallies. I shall propose a piece on this to Mr. *McCall's*.

If possible, I'd like to get you and Philip Guston together. We might even rent a car and drive up to Woodstock some afternoon. Or if he's in town, perhaps we can persuade Arthur Cohen to invite us to his Pop-Op palace uptown. I always like to combine social life with useful background material. If I am going to have to shave and wear shoes, then I want to bring back a few bits of colored glass for my notebook,—say half a dozen *choses vues*, at least.

[*Au hasard*] *Balthazar* [the Robert Bresson film] is playing around the corner. So is an old thirties serial called *Flash Gordon*, and I have to sit through hours of arty crap (e.g. a piece of pure *merde* by Polanski, Truffault's harmless but trivial early stuff, etc.) just in order to see another glorious chapter about Doctor Zarkov, the Princess Aura, Emperor Ming, Dale Arden, and dear old Buster Crabbe as desperate Flash—all of which whisk me back to my childhood as magically as Proust's madeleine.

Have you seen *The Annotated Lolita*? The original book, plus one hundred pages of footling, feeble-minded notes by an English professor named Appel (a rotten Appel indeed; a true Appel of discord). No wonder the young are burning down our universities.

. . .

*Salter's summer was divided between London and Corsica, at the invitation of the director Stanley Donen (*Two for the Road, Singing in the Rain, Bedazzled*). He worked on a film script in London, and traveled to Corsica with Donen and his girlfriend Barbara Aptekman. Phelps, meanwhile, took a cottage on Fire Island with the intention of working on a novel tentatively known as* The Silent Partner, *only to end up devoting his summer months to the care of his ailing mother-in-law, and writing journalism for immediate pay instead.*

. . .

May 20
London

Dear Robert,
Beyond the window, the tops of green trees, the center of London quiet as a garden. It's a house filled with people, and yet absolutely calm—

the ingredient, of course, is money. On the top floor are a French actress (here for a few days fitting costumes for a film), two children (Veronique and Olivia) and a maid named Celeste, teeth like dominos, wonderfully intelligent, often smiles. On my floor: me. Beneath, Stanley Donen and Mme. Somewhere further down, another maid, and in the mornings there is Hickey, the driver, *un bijou*, as they say. We sit in the kitchen drinking tea. Donen is irreverent but not cynical, he reads sections of an atrocious script someone has sent him called *Zeppelin*, typing errors and all.

Christopher: Genevieve, there's something I have to tell you. Your brother was wounded last monat. He's in a hospital in Munich.

Genevieve: How could he possible be?

Christopher: It's not serious.

It's summer. I'm working in a room the size of yours and dashing out once a day like a swallow looking for straw to see people about my film. I'll be back in early June. I read a beautiful story by Jouhandeau, "Cocu, Pendu et Content"—the arrangement of what he tells is devastating.

Absolutely no sense here of that panic which electrifies the air in New York. No rain. Hotels filled.

. . .

The British novelist Rayner Heppenstall was a favorite of Phelps. His work is thought to have prefigured the French nouveau roman but is out of print today. Seymour Krim was an American writer who has been classed both with the Beats and with practitioners of New Journalism. A book of his essays, entitled Missing a Beat: The Rants and Regrets of Seymour Krim, *was published in 2010. Glenway Wescott was a gay American novelist and a favorite of Phelps's. He was an expatriate in Paris during the 1920s, and is known for novels like* The Grandmothers *and* The Pilgrim Hawk.

. . .

May 25
New York

Dear James,
I have just looked up your *gite* . . . and am delighted to find that you are not only near Hyde Park but not far from the Brompton Oratory, where the dear wife of my erstwhile friend and hero Rayner Heppenstall used to work; not to mention La Brophy herself, who lives at 185, Old Brompton Road. Of course, this is a very subjective view of your glamorous life. I think of you going out for early walks and stopping every few minutes to make another note in one of your little books.

Here it is raining. I am working upstairs, to keep my cat company, now that Becki is at Yaddo; and this is my new Olympia typewriter, which this afternoon has to write 700 words about a friend's novel for *The NY Times*. Before or after that, I must go up to Penn Station and reserve tickets for Thursday's Metroliner to Baltimore, where, at a little after noon, I shall behold my only son taking a wife. This evening I'm dining with Glenway Wescott, to hear about his psychosomatically calcified right shoulder.

Next week I hope to start going to Fire Island. I've rented a shack on the ocean and in the most notorious of the villages, Cherry Grove: but only from Monday morning through Friday noon. So I'll miss the hanky-panky and have long solitary hours to walk by the sea and type away at my *Silent Partner* [one of Phelps's unfinished novels]. I'll be back here weekends—i.e. June 5–7, 12–14, etc. I give you dates because I don't want to miss seeing you whenever you're back. Will you be at the St. Regis again? I owe you a dinner, among other things, and of course I want to hear all about Princess Margaret.

I am reading Truman Capote in Italian (*Fra I Sentieri dell d'Eden)*—my own Berlitz method; and trying to read Updike's new book [*Bech: A Book*], which is his emptiest yet, like a row of toothpicks—plastic toothpicks, in assorted colors. And prodded by a curious piece by Seymour Krim in *The London Mag*, I've gone back to Gore Vidal, whom I hadn't tried to read for over a decade. It's not easy to see just how he differs from any other slick writer, say the guy who wrote *Airport*, etc. His essays are better, or slightly better; but I'm sure he's best at sparring with Buckley on TV.

. . .

Newell Jenkins, conductor and musicologist, was perhaps best known for presenting forgotten pieces he uncovered in European archives in his Clarion concert series. Gerald Sykes was an author and critic. He championed the works of Lawrence Durrell and Franz Kafka, among others. Buffie Johnson was an artist. Perhaps due to the timing and length of her life (1912–2006), she produced diverse works during her career, some of which could fairly be classed as surrealism, others as abstract expressionism, and still others a sort of hyperrealism. Gregory Corso was a significant figure in the Beat movement. Gasoline *(1958) and* Mindfield: New and Selected Poems *(1989) are among his major works.*

. . .

June 8
New York

Dear James,
Naked, with a glass of something called Fresca, and a fan aimed at my abdomen, I'm sitting upstairs at a very shaky cardtable strewn with cat, typewriter, mss., the proofs of Roger Straus's wife's novel (!), a Xerox of a 12-page article that must be provided with a new ending, Valium . . .

Becki adores London; wants to live there. She has become a streetwalker, talking to everyone, exhilarated at the sheer civility. Meantime Manhattan becomes measurably less bearable every day. An old friend, Philip Guston, has just returned from a winter in Italy and wants to buy a farm near Syracuse. Tonight I am baby-sitting for a couple who are moving to Spain. One evening last week I went out to dine at six.

By the time I returned, at eight-thirty, TWO for rent signs had gone up on this block. The apartment below me is available as of September 1st, the owners moving to North Africa. Newell Jenkins, next door, sets sail for Italy this week. Sunday I phoned Bella Gardner, who has an apartment at the Chelsea. It was noon. She was listening to a recording of whales with Gregory Corso. Between alcohol and an evasive black lover, she is going mad. Yesterday she began daily sessions with a new psychiatrist.

Saturday I'm to see the new Goldberg Variations ballet and then, my cat permitting, I'll go out to a swimming pool in Pound Ridge for Sunday. Meantime I must finish a memo on a book which could, but of course won't, earn me enough dollars to spend a winter in Rome.

The book I was supposed to contribute an essay on Salter to is out: mostly poor stuff, but we're both cited in an appendix, as the authors of masterworks waiting to be rediscovered.

E. M. Forster's posthumous novel was sold for $135,000 plus $100,000 from the Book-of-the-Month Club. Gerald Sykes and Buffie Johnson and Alfred Kazin's wife have left for Greece. Alfred goes to Yaddo. Ned Rorem is there at the moment, but desperate. His 1968 income tax has been challenged, and a rent inspector is demanding a look at his apartment with a view to raising it by 25%.

I think of you making tea very, very early in the morning, with heroic mists rising from your mountain meadows and "*une nouvelle page parfaite*" about to take its place in your notebook. Bless you, and your dear dog, and your indispensable children, and your precious wife—who (Yvonne Thomas assures me) is a jewel.

July 6
Aspen

Thunderstorms and hot weather. I am reading Tolstoy.

Dear Robert,

Why don't you work here? I miss you and there's nobody to speak *avec*. I may come to New York this coming Sunday (July 12th) or Monday, depending on whether [Stanley] Donen summons me or not, I've had one call but not the important one. If so, I definitely want to stay at your place, can you leave the key with the lady first floor rear? I'll likely be there Sunday–Thursday or something . . .

I saw *Bob and Alice*, which is ordinary and boring, but also *The Shadows of Our Forgotten Ancestors* (do you know this extraordinary work, made in Kiev, directed by Parajanov?) which simply alters your conception of what films can be even though it may not itself be perfect. *Ancestors* seems to me to be related to *Andrei Roublev* and even *Antonio des Mortes* which are films that directly engage themselves with myth on the highest level. Until these films and films like them are seen everywhere, we are going to be forever struggling against the kind of ignorant commercialism that defined the American 19th Century Theater, the kind that wizens us like old couples from California boarding a 747.

I've written upon and expanded (especially the opening) *To Warsaw*. Also double-spaced it because people say it seems too short. It's 147 pages now. These are the last days/weeks of hope for doing it this fall.

Love,

J.

I'm tired of my life, my clothes, the things I say. I'm hacking away at the surface, as at some kind of gray ice, trying to break through to what is underneath or I am dead. I can feel the surface trembling—it seems ready to give but it never does. I am uninterested in current events. How can I justify this? How can I explain it? I don't want to have the same vocabulary I've always had. I want something richer, broader, more penetrating and powerful. If I could only forget myself and work! That's how things are.

. . .

Maggie Smith is an acclaimed British actress, noted for her roles in The Prime of Miss Jean Brodie *and* California *for which she earned*

Academy Awards. The Norwegian actress Liv Ullmann is particularly familiar to fans of Ingmar Bergman. She has played lead roles in nine of his films, including Persona *and* Scenes from a Marriage.

. . .

July 30
London

Dear Robert,
Picasso, on hearing the news of Braque's death (Bracque?), is reported to have said only: whew.

London is cool, keen, it's rained every day as the chauffer says, not really rain, just a little weeping of the clouds. It's true it's very soft. The nights are like autumn.

We have some tickets for the *Hedda Gabler* that Ingmar Bergman directed, with Maggie Smith in the lead, and will see it tomorrow night. We screened his *Persona* yesterday, what a stunning film (I'd seen it of course—we both had) it filled me with a great sense of commitment in being a man. The paradox is—Stanley Donen talked, had dinner with Liv Ullmann in Denmark—that Bergman longs to make a film that will be a great popular success. He never has! When he sent the print for *The Passion of Anna* to America for his producers to see (UA) he received the following: We screened *The Passion of Anna* and must say we were disappointed in it. Regards. UA declined to make more of his films.

Sunday we're off to Corsica, the Donens for a month but I can't stay—I'll be there ten days or so, I expect and then begin the tortuous path home . . .

I love England. It's taken years.

August 8
Corse

Dear Robert,
Struggling among these hot stones—I don't know when I'll be back in New York, or God, even London for that matter. Everyone in Europe is on vacation, every home is empty, every hotel filled. Corsica is like

North Africa, the people seem rather small-minded, the telephone service is out of last-century China.

The Paris Review finally came out, I read my story, it seemed somehow unloving to me, perhaps that's not the word, maybe a bit ungenerous . . . It's very hard to know what you've written until some time later, you see it (if you're lucky) in print. I'd love to have your impression, please jot it down for me even if I have no address, am nowhere, at the moment. Incidentally, I will be coming through London on my way back, about two weeks from now, and can be reached . . .

I'm reading *The Sot-Weed Factor* at the moment—pressed on me by my host—which is funny but you cannot believe the length, I expect someone to tell me it was written by Barth in six weeks, I haven't had a shattering blow lately.

Great wind today. The sea is filled with whitecaps, the grasses streaming . . . I'm already promising copies of *Professional Secrets* here. We were talking last night about the immortals of film and other such foolishness. I learned that Abel Gance, whose *Napoléon* (about 1924) is said to be a masterpiece, is still shooting films (at 85) in France.

August 25
Aspen

Dear Robert,
The perfect small hotel [Hôtel Duc de Saint-Simon, Paris], I've found it for you and have a description of every room. The prices are as lovely as the little courtyard in front, they start at $3.50 and go to $14.50 for the two small apartments, I think they're 43 and 44; I'm not looking at my notes.

I didn't stop in New York on the way home. I transferred from Japan Airlines to TWA and went straight through to Denver. That was Sunday. Of course, I'm still beat. Will I ever see Europe again? I'm already thinking that, I have the guilt and insecurity of the rich . . .

Where is my *Professional Secrets*? Can you send me one? I want to have it in my hands, what does it look like? I'm going to slip into it during the cool autumn evenings as if it were a bath.

What things I have seen! Genoa at dawn—I arrived on the boat from

Corsica, the sea was like a pond, the sun not even up. I had the terrace of a little hotel high above the harbor. There were chickens strolling among the chairs and ducks nested in the garden. I have the rooms cased in this hotel, too (the Basilica). I had a room with the walls a pale blue; I felt I was in Tunisia.

My rotten tenants inform me they are leaving my Nyack house in mid-September. It will need considerable cleaning and repair; perhaps I'll do that and work in solitude, afloat in the green trees, for a month. You must see this house. I miss you.

August 28
New York

Dear Jim,
Thank you for three *echt* Salter letters, and especially for the stationery from the Saint-Simon hotel. I have assorted reasons for having not replied, the chief one being that since late July, I have been attending my mother-in-law while my poor father-in-law lay dying. All the other children were scattered—the son in Gressoney, one daughter in Dallas, my own wife at the MacDowell Colony. That's over now, and the son will have returned by next week to assume the family helm.

Prof. Secrets will go off to Aspen this afternoon. I had held your copy here, assuming you'd be coming back by way of some glamorous hotel in Manhattan. Today, in fact, is the pub. date, though the reviews will all be held up to ride tandem with Francis Steegmuller's book. I've been interviewed by nubile girls from *Time*, *Women's Wear Daily*, and yesterday I had an exquisite lunch at La Toque Blanche. I felt like someone in a Salter movie.

Today, *coıte que coıte*, I must write 750 overdue words about a book called *Yankee Doodle*, believe it or not. I'm broke. I spent $600 on a seaside pad for August, and got out there for precisely 2½ days. The ms. of my "memoir-novel" is still waiting within sound of the surf, in a suitcase along with Pavese's *Racconti*, *Thayer's Life of Beethoven*, and Stendahl's *Chartreuse*. They were to have been my late mid-summer reading.

The new *Paris Review* is still not to be had here; I check daily at the 8th Street bookshop. But I do have the re-issued paperback of *A Sport*, which I recommend *partout*.

McCall's will pay me $1,000 for a squib on Gertrude Stein, but what can I say? I visited her grave in Père Lachaise one chill, lavender January afternoon. It's between the *libres penseurs* (e.g. Oscar Wilde) and the *communistes* (Edith Piaf) in the Arab-Jewish sector, far up the ridge, beyond the crematorium and Racine and Sarah Bernhardt, with a discreetly chic headstone by Sir Francis Rose and Alice *à côté*. But would Shana Alexander's great unwashed (or rather, over-washed) want to hear merely this?

It's hot again today, but my backroom is still cool. I have a new record of Debussy's *12 Etudes*, and my cat is here, scattering black hairs on books, papers, coffee cup . . .

À bientôt; à demain.

Do come back to Nyack in October,
when the leaves will smell
good. I miss you too.

. . .

The letter Phelps refers to as looking to him as so extraordinary appears to be one of Salter's first letters to him.

. . .

September 8
New York

Dear James,
I am just back from a long weekend *chez ma belle-mère*, eating garden tomatoes under a Viking blue sky in the Bob Dylan land of what was once my hometown (Woodstock). Your letter (Harvard Club cum Brown's Hotel stationery) is one of the high water marks of my life. It inhibits and exalts me in equal proportions. It is so curious to be looked at so extraordinarily from someone else's point of view. It's like being massaged in a very posh Turkish bath . . .

This morning when I went down for the mail, there was a wad of trash, Harvey Swados's massive novel and some letters. One of them fell and as I picked it up I saw that the typed name in the upper left hand corner was "Stravinsky"!!!! As a specialist in stationery, you'll be interested to know that *le maître* uses ordinary 8½–11 typing paper and standard business envelopes. It was only a couple of lines, typed by someone else, but the immortal signature was his: wavering, elegant, inimitable, and very nearly holy, as far as I'm concerned.

No news. I'm behind in everything. Next week I go up to Peterborough to bring Becki back from the MacDowell Colony. I have three articles due by the time the sun enters Libra (circa the 21st). The ms. of my novel is in a suitcase on Fire Island, possibly washed out to sea by now. My only progress is in my fledgling Italian: I read *Gente andoggi* with my Garzanti dictionary in hand,—all about how many pairs of *scarpe* Jackie bought on Capri last week, and how the motorcycle champ Giacomo Agostino is inamorato with a French actress but doesn't promise to marry her, and of course what Walter Chiari will do now that he's out of jail for selling drugs. *Oufa*. Hug Yvonne for me.

October 2
New York

Dear James,
Exactly ten years ago today I moved to New York. I hereby declare *mon apprentissage* over. As of today, I must become a professional or perish.

Finally, yesterday, at the 8th Street Bookshop, I found a copy of *The Paris Review*. The story ["The Cinema"] is ravishing, *echt* Salter. I have read it twice; Becki has read it once . . . The thing that most gratifies me (and I mean gratify literally, as good cheese gratifies me, or a well-hung line of laundry snapping in the wind, or a Cavafy poem) is that if I stop at the end of almost any given sentence, I cannot guess what will come next—neither substance nor syntax. With most writers, there is maximum predictability. You can skim whole paragraphs. Like Isaac Babel, Salter arcs and makes right-angle turns. It is a little like riding in a flying saucer, or on the tail of a hummingbird.

But the story itself—the ambience, the details, what you tell me, is so entirely your own, and no one else's, that I find it hard to make a merely aesthetic judgment. You are a minority of one; a new herb in the cabinet; and, at the least, the most romantic writer we have. You enhance. You restore a sacredness to profaned aspects and relations. Whatever corner you are in is brightened in a grave, wistful, but unsentimental way that is *sui generis*. With wholly different temperaments, Genet and Pasolini do something of the same thing. But you are tender, and unperverse. You are pure, and in the European sense of the word, American.

. . .

The documentary director Jim Case's film The Artist in America *focused on Salter. Phelps appeared in Case's documentary to discuss Salter's work.*

. . .

October 25
New York

Dear James,
Jim Case & crew were here Friday. We tried to reach you in Piermont, but apparently you had already left. The upstairs room looked marvelous with the lights and fat cables and camera set up. Puddy (cat) was especially pleased. But I'm afraid I was lame. A camera makes me desperately uncomfortable, and besides I was pooped from two days in Boston: meeting editors, staying with friends' abundant children, getting drunk at the Ritz, walking around Walden Pond (which has an oil slick at the end where Thoreau's cottage once stood), boarding the jet shuttle in Fear & Trembling. This week I'm typing up a chapter of my novel for the *Atlantic* to consider (called "Tar Beach"); and I have a commission to do a longish piece called "In Praise of Billy Beaularis: Notes on Bisexuality." But I need material; stories. Do you know any anecdotes?

It's a good working day here, with a dark, uneventful sky and just enough rain to make the passing tires hiss on the pavement. A snug, indoor, *innerlich* day. I only wish I had a fireplace . . .

November 4
Aspen

> "To take the edge off his tension he started nipping Walker's Red Label (9:30 A.M.). By the time we were set up his 'ths' and 'eds' weren't there. Took him to the corner Italian place and filled him full of pasta. In the afternoon he was marvelous . . . " James Case

Well, Robert, there's your first, I presume, experience. You'll soon be on *The Dick Cavett Show* like Vladimir Nabokov and it will all seem a childish memory. Case is coming here once more at the end of the month and I'll find out more about it then.

This afternoon I'm going out to chop wood in the finger-biting cold. Winter is hovering above us, a week or two away. I'm struggling with one or two (absent) sentences in my Goetheaneum story which was due in September but fortunately there's no way to be late for *The Paris Review*. Next week—I have a beautiful, fresh sketch book for the purpose, one with a hard black cover—I'm finally going to start on my play. God grant it be better than some we have seen together (Why did she shoot him? Because he couldn't get a hard-on with all those (all those twenty) people watching?).

I did talk to Susan Sontag, did I tell you? I said you had seen her looking dazzling at Farrar Straus—I could feel the warmth of her reaction . . .

Would you like to visit in Aspen this winter, you Becki and Puddy? You know I have a separate house with a library, bath, fireplace, and bed on a balcony where the first light appears in small, scattered windows. Consider it.

. . .

Eduardo Sanguinetti was an Italian writer known for Alter Ego, *among other works.* Orlando Furioso *is an Italian epic poem by Ludovico Ariosto, published in 1532. Mrs. McCullers is a reference to the writer Carson McCullers, known for works such as* The Heart is a Lonely Hunter *and* The Ballad of the Sad Cafe.

. . .

November 23
New York

Dear James,
You will be pleased to know that I have lent my copies of *The Arm of Flesh* and *To Warsaw* (rev. ed.) to N., in partial repayment for lunch at the Russian tea palace and some three hours of her life saga with a Mutual Fund Man. We also talked about Mr. Salter, on whom she seems ever so slightly hung up. She has a good-looking ass (in a midi-skirt, at least) and well-spaced eyes. But she's also "into" Women's Lib a little too self-consciously and at the same time confused about whether her own "success" will clutter her femininity . . .

If an Italian production of *Orlando Furioso* comes to Aspen, don't miss it. You stand in the middle of a double basketball court and the "play" more or less erupts in three or four parts of the room simultaneously. You keep rushing around and narrowly miss being crushed by eight-foot table-platforms on wheels which are pushed at manic speed by scowling kids who don't give a damn who's in the way. Mounted on these racing tables are padded horses and glittering knights who shout glamorous Italian (Ariosto by way of Eduardo Sanguinetti). There's a hippogriff and a massive sea monster, and the Saracen siege of Paris, and a grand speech by Charlemagne on a thirty-foot tower, and a good witch and an astrologer and trapdoors and explosions (half the evening I coughed as though I'd been maced) and hordes of ardent, unwashed, warbling adorable Romans. I loved it. Part of the time I carried a four-year-old child on my shoulders and he loved it even more. At the end, the hero has gone mad (because his girl has run off with a Saracen shepherd—incidentally fellating him fiercely as the lights dimmed), and his best friend sets out on the hippogriff's back for the moon, where mad men's wits are waiting to be reclaimed. It's all called Theatre in the Surround.

I have turned down $50,000 to write a biography of Mrs. McCullers, but accepted $500 to write 625 words on an ex-press agent who makes very bad sculptures of literary people. In a small way I guess I'm a whore. Becki disapproves. So does my It, apparently. The day I was to interview the man in question I woke up deaf. An ear specialist removed a staggering quantity of wax from my ears, but looked doubtful when I suggested the crisis was psychosomatic.

Speaking of interviews, a young man came over the other evening from *Screw*—for an interview that is. He wants to be the Rex Reed of Polymorphous Perverse Sex—or so he implies. But I suspect that what he really wants to do is talk about himself. After 5 hours, including dinner and a Beethoven concert, I had done all the interviewing, so that he knew very little about me, but I knew, for instance, that he was a virgin until he was 21½ years old and that in 1968 there were only three practicing homosexuals among the student body at Cornell.

Janet Flanner is here, drinking less and looking like a chic cockatoo. She used to look like a beautiful frog prince.

No more room. I hope the play is coming. I envy you your woodchopping.

. . .

The play mentioned is one Salter had started to write, which would eventually be known as The Death Star. *Early on he feared that the play would never be produced, but it did make its way to the stage for two performances. The play dealt with the dying days of a great military commander, "a repentant one," to borrow Salter's description, and overturned the notion that such an event might stop people's urge to war. Unfortunately the play's large cast limited interest in production in New York. Despite an offer from a Los Angeles producer, Salter chose not pursue further production offers after those two performances.*

. . .

November 25
Aspen

What a flood of light a letter brings, a letter of yours. I cannot read one sentence, something about the play, oh, wait, now I see. I hope the play is coming. Well, rather painfully, it is. I have a wonderful Japanese sketchbook to write in and that's the best of it. Every morning I take off my wristwatch, read an old copy of *Le Monde* (I have hundreds) especially the literature page, and then set to work, resisting all the way, but the beginning is always difficult.

Please stop lending *The Arm of Flesh*, even to people (N.) who might like it, I don't anymore, and I must have been dizzy to imagine I once did. Yes, beneath those steel-rimmed spectacles and that terrible complexion which fascinates me, is a gleaming body, still a little new, and a ferocious hunger. But there is no linkage between the act of love and life in her, one does not flow out of the other. As you say, a beautiful ass, but it's like a beautiful car the owner doesn't know how to drive. More difficult, she is involved in this new womanhood without ever having achieved the old, not that any of us are perfectly integrated but she is visibly between personalities and, to top it off, aggressive. Still, I am interested in her life, I can't say why . . . When we're together she only tells me how feudalistic, remote and secretive I am. Is she any more generous about me when I'm not there?

My play (it's an act of rashness and a temptation to all destructive forces to begin anything without a title—the title forms the work, it's the source of endless ideas) is not quite another *Orlando Furioso*. (When it comes to Aspen—you're insane, we occasionally get a minor Benj. Britten opera, nothing more). It's a play with much that's verbal and perhaps even more that's not. If you like silences and curious passages almost like ballet, you'll like it. I'm trying to write it so it can be done with or without a stage and all the technological apparatus of modern theatre; as I said, it's appearing reluctantly at the moment, though I see before me certain stretches I am eager to reach, I hope I'm ready when the time comes.

I've ordered four copies of *Professional Secrets* and am sending them to everyone everywhere, or almost, for Christmas. What can I say except I miss you? Jim Case is arriving this coming week to do a final two days of shooting—he loves your section, he's put it all together now and says he has a nice 65 minutes.

We are opening (I'm doing the film selection and write-ups in the manner of *Cahiers*) an "art-film" theatre here beginning this Friday, two nights a week. I got them *One Plus One*, *Coming Apart*, *Fires on the*

Plain, *L'Avventura*, *Walkover* and *Ashes and Diamonds* to start. I have all my favorites coming after the first of the year. It's mildly exciting except the two men who are running it are a little lacking in fire.

You turned down $50,000 and accepted $500. I must stop thinking of you as living from hand to mouth. But where do you get your money to give you such dazzling independence?

How is your novel? Have you rescued it from Fire Island? Is the section appearing in the *Atlantic*? When?

I remember those marvelous opening lines from *Paterson*. I read Connolly several times a week, like visiting a mistress—in many ways more pleasant.

December 23
New York

Joyeux Noël . . .

I'm reading—rereading—Turgenev (*A House of Gentlefolk*); and a series of *chroniques* Colette wrote before the First World War. My own typing is ponderously blocked these days. I can't even manage letters—and I have a review that's two weeks overdue.

Meantime we've been robbed again (4th time), and I've installed $210 worth of new locks. We lost Becki's violin, the only valuable thing we possessed, as well as record player, radios, cameras, etc. If B. gets a Prix de Rome (they asked her to apply, so there's hope), I'm going to experiment with expatriation. But I may be too old to transplant.

We thought of you very tenderly the other evening while drinking a glamorous Mouton Rothschild Médoc. No interesting social life these days. The other night I had to escort Alice Morris home from a dinner party at 5th and 83rd. There were no cabs (strike) and at 2 A.M., no buses. So we had to do it by subway and hoof. Since Alice lives in the extreme west Village (the poet's Palais Royal lives in the former RCA Labs on Hudson River), it took 2½ hours.

A blizzard appears to be arriving, but in NY nothing is certain. I envy your squeaking snow. And I'm lonesome for my Woodstock fireplace of the fifties (see this month's Phelps issue of *Mademoiselle*).

WHEN ARE YOU COMING EAST?

. . .

Carlo Emilio Gadda was an Italian author. Among his best known works are That Awful Mess on the Via Merulana *and* The Philosopher's Madonna.

. . .

December 27
New York

Dear James,
Did you see that yourself and *Three* were immortalized by Mr. Rex Reed in this morning's *Times*? I have written him a letter of thanks.

This is the week of the year that most shames and aggravates me. Every time around, I promise myself that I shall treat it like a siege of pneumonia, and take proper measures. But then I lapse into ordinariness, and let myself be overwhelmed. No one to blame but Robert if I get a sulky heartburn. Life must be plotted like a Hardy novel.

On the other hand, only unwatched pots boil. Nothing is nicer than being taken unawares. As one of Isherwood's characters said when asked what in his life he was most grateful for—"Good, unexpected lays!"

Faute de mieux, I am reading eight to ten hours a day. I am even rereading Tolkien's trilogy about hobbits. When I originally read it aloud to my son, circa 1959, I wept at the end of almost every chapter. It's about courage, being chosen, the mystery of vocations; I love it. Last night, at the scene in which Frodo races the Black Riders to the fort at Rivendell, I wept again. Mysterious, since I cannot read most allegorical books, especially when they are "for children." I have never gotten through Lewis Carroll, for instance, and I loathe Kafka, except in the form of his shortest parables ("A cage went in search of a bird . . . "). In Tolkien, I think it's partly the landscaping and weather which seduce me. They are as exactly and sensuously observed as in Pavese or Colette. I can believe in the weather.

I'm also struggling to read some essays of Gadda, in Italian. What I love here is the abundance of footnotes. Someone once said that every writer has a given form, and if he never finds it, he is lost. I sometimes think mine is the footnote. For years I have dreamed of a very short story, with hundreds of footnotes appended; and when I was ten, I adored S. S. Van Dine's detective stories because they had elegantly asterisked fine print at the bottom of almost every page.

Scrapbooks, footnotes, almanacs, letters, diaries, questionnaires, marginalia, memos, alphabets . . . how I love them. Pasolini once called himself a "pasticheur." I think I am an annotator. The story exists for the scribbled notes in the margin.

How is your play?

. . .

Eva Marie Saint is an American actress famed for her roles in films such as On the Waterfront *and* North by Northwest.

. . .

December 30
Aspen

Dear Robert,
I've struggled all day with a few paragraphs and only come up with two words that make me say ah, that's interesting. It's two in the afternoon. Your letter has just arrived. I'm waiting for the strength to attempt a few pages of this unyielding play which I'm also, at last, deep into, and this evening, the single interesting touch for weeks it seems, Eva Marie Saint is coming to dinner.

Perhaps I'll come east in January . . . Meanwhile, I am continuing with *Dead Souls*, although Gogol seems to be having as difficult a time as I, and someone sent me a lovely, old, soft leather-covered copy of *Smoke* [a novel by Ivan Turgenev] which is exactly the right size to fit into my pocket and I am reading that on all the ski lifts. I hate meeting new people of which [sic] someone has not assured me "You will like them." The ski lifts are particularly dangerous in this respect.

What about your chapters in the *Atlantic*? I pray you receive the Prix de Rome, de Paris, and de London. You shouldn't fear expatriation, you've already done it, or perhaps I should say you are living in the world; literature, as we are always being told, has no boundaries.

If money comes, all will be well. Perhaps I'll go to the Chelsea, it's that time of year . . .

I really feel I've spent this year with you, at least with your spirit, which is deathless and fills me with excitement. Your existence, even in an impersonal sense, seems very important to me. When I think of you writing questions in your palms to ask the famous Agee, and reading the Italians in their own language . . .

My play, I wish I had a title, is about a third finished; not finished, but rather written down for the first time. I don't know anything about it yet except there are parts I don't detest. It has some things which astonish and some which are majestic. Anyway, as I've told you, I have a beautiful, big sketchbook in which I'm working and that's a joy.

We must consume whole worlds to write a single sentence and yet we never use up a part of what is available. I love the infinities, the endlessness involved . . .

1971 We Must Catch the Train . . .

In 1971 Phelps had not yet surrendered to the "old wounds" he refers to in one letter from that year. He was still at work on an autobiographical novel he planned to call The Silent Partner, *a reference to the strains his bisexuality had put on his marital life. Neither had he officially been diagnosed with Parkison's disease (or anything else), though the tremor that afflicted him had become a constant companion by that time. Salter attempted to distance himself from scriptwriting, completing a play entitled* The Death Star *and making preparations for a novel, which would become* Light Years.

. . .

> *Mlle. Moreau was the great French actress Jeanne Moreau. She edited an issue of* Vogue *in France, and Salter was interested in seeing it. Peter Farb was an anthropologist and writer. His book* Face of North America: The Natural History of a Continent *was so well regarded that President Kennedy presented copies to heads of state.*

. . .

January 13
New York

Dear James,
I make daily inquiries about Mlle. Moreau's issue of *Vogue*—at two local shops and *même* Rizzoli's; but it is still not available. As soon as it is, your copy will be on its way.

I met a friend of yours over the holidays—one Peter Farb. He said you are a very elegant and elusive gent.

Publishing has almost come to a stop. My agent tells me books that were accepted last fall are now being returned. Scribner's is for sale. On the other hand, I had two nice fan letters this morning, one from a girl-reporter in Washington DC: "If you're ever in the neighborhood, please stop in for a kiss on each cheek."

I am trying to finish a short story begun in 1969. My novel ground to a painful halt in December; old wounds, ancient blocks. I need new faces, fresh meat. I must go where at least the weather can be watched. New York is good only for being robbed. Almost everyone I know wants to leave. Even the girl who tends the *guichet* at the little movie house four doors away is on the wing. She has married a Frenchman and will get her French citizenship next year. Meantime she has a knife thrust at her twice a month.

Tonight I'm having dinner with a marvelous man who has a wine business in Bordeaux. He has just returned from the vendages; 1970 will have been a great year. And my beloved Janet Flanner, at 78, is about to return to the Ritz (she has a house in Orgival)—where mythic Chanel has been lying in state—to renew her NYer letter . . .

. . .

Ingo Preminger was a successful agent, film producer, and the brother of Otto Preminger, an actor, director, and producer.

. . .

January 31
Aspen

Dear Robert,
The snow is melting here, it's like summer, all the ancients are shaking their heads. I'm writing, little by little—whatever made me think I really knew what I wanted here—the missing "section" of *To Warsaw*. It's not that anyone need read it, but I am doing it as a sign of my commitment. I still expect to be back in NY on the 8th, and wondrous news: Wm. Morris has come up with some tickets to *Midsummer Night's Dream* for Friday, the 12th. There are only two. If Becki can

come, do you think you could get one or two more for that night? Two if possible. I am very excited about this and persuaded it will nourish you. If it doesn't, I won't drag you to the theatre any more until my opening which we'll celebrate like a poet's funeral. I thought of you this morning, took courage, and threw away two unworthy books. I'm working today (Sunday) after having spent yesterday skiing with Ingo Preminger (*M.A.S.H.*) and listening to descriptions of a little farmhouse he's bought and will soon be going to in Bad Ischl, surrounded by the bluest of lakes. Did I tell you that he received not long ago, a check for $1,300,000 as his share of the profits on *M.A.S.H.*? We paid for our own lunches, however.

March 5
New York

Dear James,
The story ["Am Strand von Tanger"] is *echt* Salter. Did you make up that marvelous detail about your hero being born on the day Gaudi died? My Petit Larousse says it was 1926. I love the "senseless" mouth. How many short stories do you have? Enough for a book? The two I know are extraordinary, *sui generis*; you are an original. Good lord, send me the one with the Grotowski title, please! How can you even ask? You are the only contemporary writer I know whose work I entirely revere, am even in awe of, and can never quite predict. Your *mots* are not only *justes* but unforeseeable by me. *Tu m'étonne*, really.

Since our evening with Shakespeare, I've seen it again; and wept again. What glamour of language, and what tender, tart, forbearing knowledge of human nature. (Do you know his great line—from *Winter's Tale*: "I have drunk, and seen the spider . . . "?).

Yesterday we had manic winds, along with sleet, snow, glintings of sunlight and bitter cold. I could hardly stay indoors. Eventful weather is so rare in New York. The girl upstairs had a window blown in—like *Wuthering Heights*.

All my fingers are crossed. I cross them whenever I think of you. I want to write something about you making a film. I even have the title—*Hardness 8*. (Diamonds are measured on a scale of one to eight). But my God, magazines are vanishing every day. Willie Morris has resigned from *Harper's*—apparently *à cause de* Mailer, or that silly, sloppy article which I lost interest in (the sentences as well as the ideas) by the third page. And *New York Magazine* is in trouble, I'm told. I scribble and scribble—this month for *Mlle* and *Vogue* (twice) and *Life*. For *Mlle*, I have to do 2,500 words on "female sexuality." Please send me two or three anecdotes, huh? I'll try to contrive a reference to *A Sport*. Speaking of which, Monday evening, before my New School workshop, I was sitting in the Bambino restaurant, browsing over chapter 19 (with that beautiful first paragraph) and I realized that the couple at the table could be out of a Salter story. He drank Perrier water as well as red wine. He talked slowly, authoritatively about "a condominium in St. Tropez," a new apartment he was buying, a girl who "had gotten into bed with me last night" and who turned out to be his 3-year-old daughter. The wife listened, nibbled absently, spoke very little, accepted the elegant shirt and even more elegant cuffs.

Twenty-eight of Becki's paintings were shipped to Duke University yesterday. I helped load them, like so many small sailboats in that gale. Once I almost rose into the air.

Someone gave us a television set last week, and so I've had a look at what America has been doing for twenty years. (I always come late. I am the tortoise). It's bleaker than I thought. Even the "old" movies. My God, who can see Merle Oberon in the *Cowboy and the Lady*, or Louis Jordan in *Decameron Nights*? It's insane. The only things I haven't been dismayed by are Joe Louis' face, and Julia Child, who must have emphysema but whom I can't help loving . . .

It's March 5th. I have to write a book review, due two weeks ago. (I am not only a tortoise, I am a tormented tortoise).

Next door, Newell Jenkins is playing a recording of my favorite piece of 19th century music, Rossini's *Petite Messe Solennelle*: as sexy as *La Traviata*. And did you know this: the Princess Natalie Paley, who in the early 30s aborted a child by Jean Cocteau (!), was once married to the courtier Lucien Lelong, whose later wife (and widow) Sanda

Dancovici, was eventually (in the late 50s) to marry Colette's 3rd husband, Maurice Goudeket?

Now I must go up to East 51st and have lunch with Glenway Wescott, whom I haven't seen since late 1970. No wind today and the sun is bright and warm.

. . .

Carl Ruggles was an American composer known for Sun-Treader, *among other compositions. Barbara Rosenthal is the wife of composer Laurence Rosenthal and the probable model for Nedra in Salter's novel* Light Years. *Monroe Wheeler was the writer Glenway Wescott's companion for many years and a longtime board member of the Museum of Modern Art.*

. . .

March 15
New York

Cher Jeem,
Enclosed is one of your old girlfriends [Charlotte Rampling, star of *Three*], as of last week's *l'Expresso*. She looks liberated.

Send me Barbara Rosenthal's address, please, so I can mail her your copy of *Prof. Secrets*.

Almost sixty degrees F. here today, with high wind, thunderheads, intoxicating sunshine, after days of smog. Last week I lost my balance—literally—for three days. My doctor diagnosed a bacterial infection of the "middle ear." (I have three, you know). There's a proper name—Labyrinthitis. I couldn't stand up. The room reeled, and once I fainted, just like Pearl White. Since then I've had a physical exam and all seems okay. No Parkinson's disease yet, though my sigmoidoscopy is yet to come.

I'm reading Virgil Thomson's new book . . . *American Music Since 1910*. I must send you a copy. The chapter on my old hero Carl Ruggles (who was 95 last Thursday) is one of the best things I've ever read on being American and trying to create.

I've also read [Francis] Steegmuller's biography of Cocteau, which has lots of interesting minutiae about the twenties, but whose point of view is too patronizing (at best) and helplessly, hopelessly scornful for me. Steeg is a Victorian man. He should have a Scout troop. But in spite of him, dear, silly, narcissistic, wise, intelligently kind Cocteau comes through. Colette once said "*Jean est triste parce qu'il est bon.*" And Monroe Wheeler, who knew him for decades, says he was one of the kindest men he's ever met. "Meeting you after a year, he would promptly quote something you had said, pronounce it delicious, and even better, go on convincing you that it had been so, thus leaving you refreshed, grateful, happy to be yourself."

Money. I'm trying to think of how to eat for two years without article-writing. My latest daydream is to be called *An Alphabet of Great American Myths*. Mae West, Johnny Appleseed, Mickey Mouse, Elsa Maxwell, Man-O-War, Charles Lindbergh, Kilroy, Nathan Hale, Red Grange, Charles Ives, Diamond Jim Brady, Loeb & Leopold, Buffalo Bill, Ahab, Tom Paine, "Old Ironsides," Frankie and Johnny, etc. Two or three-hundred—all recreated by my prose in squibs from two lines to two pages, à la Bulfinch. Not statistics, but emblematic gestures, acts.

Interrupted by the arrival of Auden's bibliographer from Yale University, who wants to interview me on the master!

. . .

First Love *was a film based on a novel by Ivan Turgenev and directed by Maximilian Schell. It was nominated for an Academy Award for Best Foreign Language Film.*

. . .

March 18
New York

Dear James,

I have decided to memorize a poem every week. It's something to repeat to oneself when standing in the subway, and then too, it keeps the remembrance muscle firm. I'm beginning with "L'Albatros" of Baudelaire.

Auden's bibliographer has just been here again. A young owl from Yale who would be tedious without his obsession. As it is, I find him fascinating, since he is the only other person I have ever known with whom I could gossip about Auden's book reviews. We are like two eleven-year-old Red Sox fans talking statistics. Insane but tonic.

I'm typing this note to warm up for my 600 words on Erik Satie. I've read what Stravinsky said about him, and Poulenc, and Virgil Thomson, and John Cage, and of course Cocteau, and now I have to make a valentine (for *Vogue*). Did you know that after he died, his friends found one hundred unused umbrellas in his room? There was also a piano, which was unplayable and which Braque bought as a souvenir.

I saw *First Love* last night, and was surprised at how anyone could make such a soft, pretentious muddle out of such a lean and supple piece of story-telling (Turgenev's that is!). And what a pathetic abuse of poor Dino Lipatti! I suppose *Elvira Madigan* was released the week the soundtrack was being fixed up. So many promising ingredients wasted. And the girl simply could not act. (She also looked as though she had a hare-lip, though of course she didn't).

Are you in good spirits? Are you losing patience with everyone? I have promised myself to get out of Manhattan by June 20th. But where the hell can I go? I want sea air, sun, a decent newsstand, a place for my cat to glower at birds, a place I don't have to cook, a place my wife can occasionally visit me, a place I won't need a car, etc. etc. Preposterous. A friend of mine goes to Hydra the Greek island and works very well there, at one third of the cost of Springs, or Maine, or Ischia. Another friend has recommended a Danish nudist colony. Like all Scorpios, I am totally passive about terrestrial movements.

Auden has written Stravinsky's obituary for the *Observer* to have ready. Did you see the long excerpts from Robt. Craft's diary in the *NY Rev. of Books* last month?

March 22
Los Angeles

Dear Robert,
We are into the final hours.

Until today I thought we would get the money [to make *To Warsaw*] from Canada. The company liked the film but in the end it didn't qualify under the general rules that permit government subsidy (which is where the money comes from).

I've been in California all week. The results haven't become known yet. It's being read in two places in London and two more in New York. If we don't have it financed by the end of the month, I'm afraid it will mean the end.

In San Francisco, American Zoetrope which is Francis Coppola's pop-art production center, liked it instantly. They've sent it to Coppola himself (at present girding for three months of Marlon Brando) for his approval. Unfortunately, they have no money, but they might give us free post-production. That's all right provided we have something to post-produce.

I also found someone who will distribute it. It's only the rest we lack.

. . .

The book Salter refers to as "Aubrey's Lives*" is John Aubrey's* Brief Lives (1669–1696).

. . .

March 23

Last night, still somewhat dazed from travel, I went to look at a girl named Lauren Hutton in *Little Fauss and Big Halsy* but wound up in the wrong movie by mistake and saw *Catch-22* again. It didn't seem as long the second time but many of the routines weren't worth a second look.

Your idea about the Great American Myths—do you know Aubrey's *Lives*? Astonishing, eclectic, singular book, filled with some things that are obviously so true they penetrate one like a line of Donne, and other things that are merely outrageous gossip, but how it all lives . . . I still read your literary scrapbook—how crude of me—your chart of the heavens every morning, it extends me, it is my first breath.

What would you think of a book which reveals, derives, and attempts to place in a certain order or state of superimposition the mythical systems and signs which foretell everything? I mean the phenomena and the theories, like sunspots, yes, of course, stars, graphology, parapsychology, clothing (length of skirts), superstition, electro-magnetic forces, etc., etc., but using everything, from all the world, oriental, black African, everything. A geography of the unknown but deeply suspected, a chart of undefined forces, a sort of encyclopedia—atlas—handbook, beautifully documented and arranged, of all that we realize must have some substance but which is indicated only by oblique, even primitive, means.

I am living two lives, I must abandon one, but I'm afraid if I put myself entirely in one it won't support me, it will give way.

Robert, you know I love you. I want you to live in Italy, to be free. The chances become slimmer that we will go together.

April 17
Aspen

Dear Robert,
The beasts are lying in the sun, their nostrils quivering as they smell the new air. I am working like a scrubwoman, I see nothing, I hear nothing. Did you dislike that story so much or did it disappoint you so that you look at me in a different, lesser way? Not a word from you for weeks. Meanwhile clods of earth have been tumbling onto *Warsaw*. No one will put up the money. We hold a mirror before its mouth to see if it's still breathing.

I'm trying to sell my house in Nyack. The agents are already leading suburban couples through it. I have to come east to do the last repairs and make everything nice. I expect it will be at the end of next week (the 25th).

The Colette of Aspen—Dee Vare is her name, she lives in a collection of shacks that are beautiful inside with a failed architect who makes furniture now, chairs, lovely tables—adores your books, I put her on to them, she has a hammock in a little garden behind her house and is usually stoned at noon. Fabulous teeth, the eye of a gypsy. I love your friend, she says.

On the 15th of May, as into icy waters, I plan to begin the rewriting of this play and finish at the end of June. It will still be incomplete, but at least there will be something to see then.

April 21
Pound Ridge

Dear James,
I loved the story ["Via Negativa"], and am ashamed I have taken this long (I had an attack of labyrinthitis—acute dizziness due to an unhappy "middle ear"!)—to acknowledge it. I read it aloud to Becki the morning it arrived and she pronounced it her favorite Salter story yet. It's as precise and stately as an orrery. Next Monday I'm having tea with Bill Maxwell, an editor at the *NYer*, and I'll take it along. Naturally it isn't for *Paris Review*, what with those hand-made shoes and all.

I'm upstate 30 miles (a town called Pound Ridge, about which I only know that it's somewhere near Purchase, where our publisher Roger S. lives). I needed some fresh air, having thoroughly fouled up the atmosphere of my well shaft. Besides I have an article that must be finished (due two weeks ago and I need the dollars it will bring in). It's quiet here, with starlight coming in the window next to my bed, and marvelous food. Yesterday I saw some red-tailed hawks mating in the sky—crying out, soaring, planning, and then coming together. The gardener here, named Jason, said they only do it on days of high wind. Then they nest in rock outcroppings and lay the eggs.

I was up at 6 this morning. Two cups of coffee and four holograph pages of my *Silent Partner*. Then breakfast at nine—melon, poached eggs, fantastic bacon, and an extraordinary lecture on chinaware from my hostess. (Did you know that ironstone dishes were manufactured for export to America—in the 18th century—to be used as ballast on ships carrying tea? The exporters wanted a profitable ballast, and of course the unfashionable colonists didn't need Wedgewood or Haviland, after all. That's how history books should be written). At nine-thirty back to my room and five typed pages of my article. It's crap but has a great quotation from Sir Thomas Browne: "Epicurus himself found Jupiter's brain in a piece of Cytheridean cheese, and the tongues of nightingales in a dish of onions."

My hostess is an old friend of Philip Roth, who used to come here to write *Portnoy*. She tells me he puts the ms. of his current book in the refrigerator every day—in case of a fire.

This afternoon I'm going to saw up a dead apple tree downed by the wind last January. I'll be back in NY on Friday morning. Phone as soon as you get to Nyack. We must eat some oysters before the months without an "R"; and we must drink some Scotch to Igor S., whose music I have been playing incessantly since April 6th.

. . .

Story Theatre *was written by Paul Sills. Its aim was to present productions focusing on story, often in the sense of fairy tales, rather than standard dramatic productions. John Collier was a British author. Many of his stories appeared in* The New Yorker *during the 1930s, 1940s, and 1950s.* An American Girl *(1969) was a novel by Patricia Dizenzo. Paul Scofield was to star in and Schell to direct a film Salter had written for Robert Ginna called* The Blue Clown.

. . .

May 16
Aspen

Dear Robert,
I think I'm going to stop my trips to New York. I'm out of money, for one thing, though I daily expect someone to buy or at least seriously admire my house—I will roll in that money, I will canter in it, I will never let it go. Secondly, I never see enough of you and when I do, I

bring the wrong spirit, one of noise and movement, I'm always late. I want to float in the deeps with you, not splash loudly near the beach.

Your letters awaited me, including the beautiful chart which I can't read but, like an illiterate, I prize. I also had a lovely letter from John Collier, who was seventy this month. His letter bears no reference to time, does not acknowledge it. He writes as if he had always been part of the world and always would be.

Another thing, I'm not going to any more plays. I walked out of the *Story Theatre* after the first act. If I can't see things as good as I dream my own will be, then nothing. In Denver, what a city, clean, juiceless as Queens, streets empty at six at night, dying people and cars, I saw *Lawrence of Arabia*, it was for the first time. Wonderful film, of course, I didn't believe it, it was like Shaw, but still wonderful. And marvelous to look at. Yesterday I read *An American Girl*. Tomorrow I'm going to work. Apparently I'll have about four weeks here and then, if things go well, to England and see Scofield and Schell. I must be concerned about it or at least filled with a kind of broth of it, last night I dreamed about Max Schmeling.

I'm afraid this letter will be too late for Becki, so will you send it on to her?

There is the lovely sound of my daughter's horse grazing near me. I expect to see you emerge from the haze of this summer with great things in your refrigerator.

May 19
Aspen

Dear Robert,
Quiet morning, I feel I am on vacation, on Bergman's silent island. Occasionally every part of the day seems sublime, as if I am passing from one mature pleasure to another. I'm sleeping alone in the studio which is lovely and cool (my wife has a bad cold). The neighborhood children are all at school. In the afternoons, I turn to carpentry where one really accomplishes something. Becki received my letter—that's good. She sent me a card. I'm enclosing some ads from *The London*

Times of April 1927 which I had intended to send, too. The description of these hotels in the days before England became mean, democratic, and poor is delicious. A kind of beautiful, English boredom falls upon me, I long to have lived in those years, to have been proper, had a country house, traveled to Scotland. We must catch the train, Robert, we must move, otherwise life takes you, makes you soggy. We're wearing cheap shoes, we must stay ahead of it. I am running and then falling abruptly with/in my play, like a drunken man alone on the beach. Oh, there are marvelous things I am eager to get to, but one must not hurry, one must pay for the coming moment. No news, none at all, from New York or the Great Life Beyond. I have a birthday coming which I face with the equanimity of Sophocles. It is bitter but I hardly taste it. I'm having tea in the sunshine. I wish we were together.

May 24
New York

Dear Jim,
Pier 44, or the old ferry landing at the foot of Christopher Street, is a sort of mini-park. You can dangle your legs over the Hudson, which is majestic no matter how soiled, and watch the gulls, and the Statue of Liberty, and an occasional boat. Yesterday was lovely and I sat a modest quarter of a mile out into the river for three hours, hugging two or three dogs that tumbled beside me and talking with Ed Hoagland. Do you know his work? *The Courage of Turtles* has some beautiful pieces which for lack of a better word we have to call "essays." He once worked in a circus (source of his novel, *Cat Man*) and saw a man's arm snapped off by a Bengal tiger. This summer he goes to the White/Green mountains, to write a nature book for *Time/Life* (@$18,000). He stutters, and dresses with a winningly old-fashioned non-coquetry (loose, unselfconscious; oblivious). Rampant with allergies, so he can't keep his own dog except in the summer, in the country. But a very good writer, I think. I told him about *Sport*, and your ears should have tingled.

They might also have tingled Saturday night, when I had dinner with Our Yvonne and we talked about not only *Sport*, but *Three*, your horoscope, and the Salter Mystery in general. She's looking fine; just back from Paris (I think she stayed at the Montelambert, or maybe it was the Pont-Royal, so remember to ask her if she saved any stationery for your collection); and should be in Aspen early in June by way of East Hampton. I love to be with her; I wish we had had an affair twenty years ago. She has temperament. She's memorable, and ever so slightly cuckoo in a way I adore.

Thank you for the letter to Becki. You are almost the only friend I have whom she genuinely likes, even loves. (Of course so many of the others are queer, or semi-demi-queer, which tires her—literally, I mean: she falls asleep when they're here. The last time Glenway Wescott was here, she fell asleep while he was reading from his new story).

Thank you also for the sentence beginning "We must catch the train, Robert, we must move . . . " I've typed it out and pinned it on my bulletin board. It came on exactly the right morning. I woke up groggy, sulky, unharnessed, with a day of chores ahead: a squib for *Life* on Wm. Maxwell's book, my last class at the New School (I loathe farewell performances), a memo to write for my agent—and about a book I don't want to do, etc. Your admonition reminded me that there are delights waiting, Albanian freighters to Tunis, et al.

Yvonne invited me to Aspen but I can't make it this summer. I'm going to Provincetown (the NON-Mailer end) in August, and if my book isn't finished, to the MacDowell Colony in October (where you can walk hip-deep in red and yellow maple leaves). Speaking of Mailer, did you see my pen-pal Brophy's straight-arming of him in yesterday's *Times*? It's wonderful to know you, to look forward to 1980, 1990.

. . .

The Last Analysis *was a play of Saul Bellow's, not one of his major works, but of interest to Salter at the time, as he had just completed* The Death Star, *his first play.*

. . .

August 16
Aspen

Dear Robert,

Dinner with Saul Bellow at Yvonne's. I was afraid to say anything to him. A writer, a real writer, I kept thinking. I did ask him about *The Last Analysis*. He wrote it side by side with *Herzog*, he said, encouraged by a $5000 grant arranged for him by Lillian Hellman. She hated it when she saw it—because it wasn't well-made, he said. Anyway, no more theatre for him, the people are all too foolish, he says.

I'm fifteen pages from the end and hate my play. With all my strength, the other day, so heavy with depression I was panicky, I couldn't think, I couldn't hope, I managed to write on a piece of paper "Go to the End" and put it in the manuscript as a sort of bookmark.

Eighty degree days, the sun is naked here . . . September is coming, and skies of the deepest, most burning blue imaginable. I hope to begin a book and if I live through the winter, well, not finish it but at least have something. I saw a story by your friend Edw. Hoagland in *The New Yorker* but haven't read it. *NAR* [*The New American Review*] turned down "Via Negativa," they said it wasn't "overwhelming enough." Come out, I am dying.

. . .

Andrew Lytle was a writer. Notable among his works is the novel The Velvet Horn. *The "old friend" who asked Phelps to translate his novel* Un Eternel Amour de Trois Semaines *into English was the writer Jean Chalon. Phelps did not translate the book. Marcia Nardi was a poet, better known for appearing in William Carlos Williams's* Paterson *than for her own work. Allen Tate was a member of the Fugitive Poets and later the Southern Agrarians. He was also an essayist and the author of one novel,* The Fathers.

. . .

August 19
New York

Dear, dear Jim,
Don't die; I need you; so does your dear dog, not to mention countless suppliers of stationery to the better European hotels. I am reading the early stories of Carson McCullers. The very first, called "Sucker," was rejected by 26 magazines and it's very good. If you have no better place to send "Via Negativa," try *The Sewanee Review*. The editor is Andrew Lytle, himself a fine writer. Tell him I urged you to send it. We're old confreres, i.e. we have reviewed each other's books. The pay is small but the ambient is not undistinguished. What readers you get are serious and take you seriously. Furthermore, the magazine is not pulped, like *Vogue* or *Esquire*, but bound and preserved in libraries. If you do send it, address the envelope to Andrew personally, at Assembly Grounds, Monteagle, Tennessee. *The Review* offices are at the University of the South, but may be closed in August. Andrew is an honorable man. His neighbor is Allen Tate, who is now married to an ex-nun and, at seventy, making babies regularly. He too is an honorable man . . .

As for my mail, your own letter has been the only decent thing in it since you were in London. From California, sulky Anaís Nin writes that she is "naturally disappointed that you never wrote about them (her diaries) as you said you would" etc. From Marblehead, manic Marcia Nardi sends special delivery letters about her gall bladder operation (sic). From Paris, an old friend sends me proofs of his new novel (called *Un Eternel Amour de Trois Semaines*), asking me to translate it, please(!), and if I feel that "*les passages sur l'astrologue et le personnage de Rene* (presumably based on me) *te gêne, supprime-les*."

My only joy is my son. In Firenze, he is wildly happy, eating melons, taking a crash course in Italian, and advertising himself in the local paper as "*Enseignero la lingua Inghlese*." He wants to live in Toscana forever, and asks me to forward his wife's hair drier as soon as possible . . .

. . .

Robert Silvers, about whom Saul Bellow told Salter stories, helped found the New York Review of Books *and edited it for many years.*

. . .

September 2
Aspen

Dear Robert,
Well, I finished the play—almost—it's at the typist's, I'm sure there will be some terrible things in it I've never even read. Your letter brought me to life for the final, staggering assault. I haven't tried *The Sewanee Review* because the story is still at *Transatlantic*. I hope it has a long rest there. I'm tired of picking it up. If it comes back, I'm going to write a long letter to Andrew Lytle which I intend to make so impressive with perfectly placed references to you that he won't be able to refuse.

In the meantime, Saul Bellow has been here and gone. We had frequent dinners, all without contact. He tells people he likes me, I don't know what to make of him. He knows so much, that's one thing that puts me off, and also I know my betters. He told a story about an Hungarian count who is obliged to tell his son about the birds and the bees. He told about Rob't Silvers in Israel, about his cousin, Glinka, he's very witty (Saul), looks like a tortoise, has quite a large smile. Yvonne is cool at the moment, I'd like to have her opinion with all its confusion. I tried to find a cabin for him next year, he wanted more isolation and silence. We drove about eight miles into the woods and looked at one by the Roaring Fork near a ruined bridge where the stagecoach once crossed. Of course, there was no electricity. He turned it down because the sound of the diesel generator was too loud (you couldn't hear it inside the house). It was the princess and the pea, but then he told some very winning stories on the way back . . .

. . .

The Blue Clown *was a script Salter had written several years earlier. The director Sidney Lumet expressed interest in it, but Salter was not convinced the script and director would be a good pairing. Lumet was familiar with Salter's work after directing* The Appointment, *a film based on a script Salter originally wrote for Peter Glenville. "I can't think of a more imperfect union than that of Sidney Lumet and this particular script, or any of mine for that matter," he told Phelps. Ultimately the film was not produced. Cynthia Buchanan was a writer, best known for her novel,* Maiden. *Terrence McNally is a decorated American playwright, known for works such as* Frankie and Johnny in the Clair de Lune *and* Lips Together, Teeth Apart.

. . .

September 10
Aspen

Dear Robert,
I often think about those lines of Conrad's about finishing his book and taking the train to London, where he had sent his wife and child. What became of that child? I've sent you my play, above all because of your demonstrated passion for the theatre. Now, I know what will happen: a month will pass and I will receive a letter saying, oh, yes, that, that . . . Becki loved it. Please don't do this. I know the play is imperfect, but even Terrence McNally had a beginning.

Gwenn, Yvonne's youngest, came by yesterday to borrow a knapsack. It absolutely astonished me how much she was like her mother—her gestures, her very words. Yvonne has lost her studio, which was in a marvelous, old building in the center of town (it's being "redone") but I think she's soon for New York anyway. I am for oblivion unless I get a Guggenheim or R. E. Ginna, Jr. manages to produce *The Blue Clown*. I'm so sick of the script I cannot believe anyone will be fooled, but apparently it has some power to confuse because Scofield is still there and even Max Schell who says he will come to NY himself in three weeks to sell it shoulder to shoulder with Ginna. I have twenty or twenty-five thousand dollars due me if it's ever made, I'll get a divorce and live by the sea.

How to describe a book I intend to write for the Guggenheim Selection Committee—I am not even sure myself of what it will be, I intend to unearth it, all I know is its mass, its density, it lies beneath the surface and makes compasses erratic? Well, I am not wondering anymore "what other people do." I'll tell them as much as I know. I expect them to turn me down.

I can't seem to do anything now that the play is finished. My limbs are heavy. I can't even be amused, well, not easily. I sit in a little, gravel garden with a board across two stumps which is my table and dream of all I have to do, none of which seems worth it. There is one small apple-tree in this garden, it's managed to live for a year despite everything, probably because I sit so close to it and the body warmth . . . It may survive, but there's no possibility of my ever sitting in its shade.

My daughter has gone to Rome with Barbara Rosenthal—it's for the year if it works out and she can get into a school. One of the Rosenthal *filles* will be in Wales at the university, the other at home. *Père* Rosenthal is doing the music arranging and recording for *Man of La Mancha*, the work which future generations will probably judge us by.

When do you go to Yaddo?

Are you allowed visitors? For lunch, say?

I hope women gain their freedom, Cynthia Buchanan included.

. . .

Bob Craig wanted Salter to write a script for a mountain-climbing movie. The script was completed but was never filmed. It would eventually, however, serve as the foundation for Salter's novel Solo Faces. *Salter also mentions Christo, who worked with his wife, Jeanne-Claude, on massive public art projects. Jeanne-Claude died in November of 2009.*

. . .

September 12
Aspen

Dear Robert,
That hour when, by the sea, the sun seems to burn without heat, the wind rises, and the noise too. Aspen is empty. I've done nothing all day but read and throw away old copies of *Le Monde*, I love its confidence, its grand style, its assumption that many things are so, taken for granted, understood. And, of course, its wonderful pages on literature.

Last night Bob Craig came with several beautiful books on mountain climbing. He was on the ill-fated 1953 American expedition to climb K-2 (the second highest in the world, the mountain of mountains, they call it). They were at 25, 26, 27,000 feet for weeks without oxygen. The weather turned against them. One of them became critically ill (blood clots in the lung) and in the effort to save him, to bring him down, everything collapsed. And in the end, he was killed by an avalanche anyway, the sick man, no trace, nothing, ever. Craig wants to make a great mountain film. He wants me to write it. He doesn't know I dream of spending my life in the theatre and never even seeing a movie again.

I had one piece of good news. The O. Henry has taken another story, "The Destruction of the Goetheanum," for its 1972 edition. This means that sometime in 1973 I'll get a check for $126. Imagine, I don't even know this editor and he's taken two stories—demolishes our theory.

Not a word yet from my daughter in Rome, though her boyfriend bicycled by me on the street today and said he'd had three. Yvonne leaves for New York on Wednesday, suddenly as she says. There was a party for her at Herbert Bayer's—he's an ex-member, I should say he was a Bauhaus member and is the town's only painter—and an artist named Cristo (sp?) was there. He's from Bulgaria and New York, very nice, French wife, who is engaged in putting up a two-mile curtain, as I understand it, across a valley at Rifle (about 45 miles from here). I didn't ask why, but Yvonne said it was a marvelous concept. Cristo's wife is Parisienne. Yvonne said: I am from Nice—forty-four years! Did

I ever tell you the story of her humiliation when she was returning to France after the war with nylons and radios and other contraband, much of it concealed on her person, and she was searched and caught by French customs?

I am too weak to continue. Tomorrow I'm starting that dreadful autobiographical essay which accompanies the Guggenheim application. I must get all that done this week.

Are you well?

Contento?

. . .

Peter Deane coauthored The Literary Life: A Scrapbook Almanac of the Anglo-American Literary Scene from 1900 to 1950 *with Robert Phelps. Bianca VanOrden is the author of* Fire Music, *among other works. Robert Gorham Davis was professor emeritus at Columbia University. As a critic, he concerned himself with John Dos Passos, among others, and published short fiction of his own in* The New Yorker. *Mark Schorer was a critic and writer. In addition to an influential study of Sinclair Lewis, Schorer's fiction was published in* The New Yorker *and* Esquire.

. . .

September 13
New York

Dear James,
The play has not yet arrived, but the heralding letter came this morning and was read and relished three times through as I sipped my coffee and listened to Stravinsky's wind concerto. Becki is at Yaddo until tomorrow and Peter Deane was here for the weekend. Since he loves *Sport* almost as much as I do, I read him the letter and you were severally savored.

I go to MacDowell (in Peterborough, New Hampshire) on October 1st. It's then or never. I have been so clenched and unproductive this year that even I am amazed. I'll have 6 weeks. I must spurt something out, and get the mess I call my manuscript into shape—any shape. What I yearn to write is a very short lyric narrative, say 30 pages, with about 250 pages of happy footnotes, into which I can cram all my marginalia. I am very Alexandrian, I guess—all margin and barely any text. As a child I loved S. S. Van Dine's detective stories because they sometimes had as many as four footnotes at the bottom of a page. I was doting on the notes to "The Waste Land" long before I had any understanding or respect for the poem itself. And to this day the notes to Auden's "New Year Letter" remain one of my dearest "reads." My favorite contemporary Italian writer – Alberto Arbasino – has a novella called *Il Ragazzo Perduto* with 178 footnotes, and when I found out that he, in turn, had caught the bug from Carlo Emilio Gadda's *L'Adalgisa*, I felt like Schliemann at the 9th level of Troy. I promptly ordered a copy, which came months later from a Florentine bookseller's cellar, where it had barely survived the Flood. Waterlogged and mud-stained, it nevertheless cost me $25!—and though my Italian isn't agile enough to get me through it, I revel eagerly in the footnotes.

It rains and rains. I spent the Labor Day weekend in the country, at Glenway Wescott's house in western New Jersey, on the Delaware River. Fresh peaches and sweet corn and the best martinis I have ever known (Tanqueray gin—four whopping beakers to a dash of Noilly Prat, and a very thin wafer of lemon rind). Glenway was away but his longterm consort Monroe Wheeler was there, as well as the millionaire sister-in-law Barbara and hundreds of rolling acres of prize cattle. My cat vanished the morning I was to return, so I had to stay on another day. It's a wonderful house—18th century fieldstone, with imported floors from an old French manor, and thousands of books, and paintings everywhere. Because of the recent rains, the lawns were violently green, but strewn already with tiny yellow leaves from the walnut trees. I browsed and read and lay in the sun and talked with Monroe, who is the toughest, most empirical, worldly man I've ever known. He, in turn, had just returned from a week in Maine, with Brooke Astor and Laurence Rockefeller's yacht. It rents for $2,000 per diem, if you're interested. Sleeps 16 and there's a French chef. He tells marvelous stories and I'm trying to persuade him to write his memoirs.

I am supposed to write a book review of Forster's posthumous novel for *Life*, but I can't seem to do it. I'm sick-sick-sick of hackwork. I've done nothing else all year. *Mlle* for this month has my squib on astrology and sex and the sight of it almost makes me dizzy. I should have been a land surveyor and never tried to earn my living by my typewriter. This moment I am editing a pilot sampler of 150pp. out of Glenway's diaries, letters, obiter scripta, etc. for 1955. It's to go to Roger Straus, who wants to commission me to prepare 4 volumes of Wescott journals. It's like playing with paper dolls—all scissors and paste, with several colors of ink. I do it three hours every afternoon, and the only bad part is the temporary illusion it gives of covering pages. Alas, they're someone else's and as so often, I'm just a bridesmaid.

I'm applying for the Gugg. too, though I don't think that disqualifies me for writing a letter about you. I have applied three or four times since 1959 but always been rejected. Jim Agee was rejected 9 times, and his sponsors included Auden, John Huston, etc. Wm. de Kooning was rejected 11 times. It is said you are always rejected the first time, on principle, but I know a girl named Bianca VanOrden who is at least one exception to that rule. When Susan Sontag was turned down in 1965, I think, she howled so long and so loud that Robt. Lowell picked up his cane and went around to the Rockefeller Foundation (he had forgotten which one she had been rejected by) and banged on the director's desk and they gave her $8,000 on the spot. (The next year the Gugg. came across too).

I started to apply last fall but then got discouraged because I couldn't think of three good sponsors. Dear old Louise Bogan had offered (in fact had done so on my three previous applications), but died. Glenway is too maverick to impress Gugg. judges. Professors are best, but I know only Robt. Gorham Davis, who is as mild as a hare, and Mark Schorer, who offered but who has only moderate enthusiasm about my p-r-o-s-e. I suppose I could flatter Anaís Ninny until she put me in the next volume of her Journal. I've thought of forging a paragraph in French and signing it Colette, but she died in 1954. *Enfin* . . .

Saul Bellow would be the ideal sponsor for you. He's the perfect combination of Town and Gown, Class and Mass, Mind and Matter, etc.

What do you mean "divorce"? Do you realize we never confide anything about our imperfect lives to each other?

I'll mail *Heroes and Orators* as soon as I can get it into a jiffy bag—for which I must go to a stationer's on Broadway—and then to the PO. Meantime I'm starting a commune (of which more later).

. . .

Lucian Freud is a painter, known for works such as Benefits Supervisor Sleeping, *the most expensive painting ever sold by a living artist. His work is controversial and prized, his portraits in particular. The grandson of Sigmund Freud, he is an elusive figure, rumored to have dozens of illegitimate children. One of Robert Lowell's wives, Elizabeth Hardwick, was a writer and cofounder of* The New York Review of Books. *She was well regarded as an essayist, and she was the author of three novels, one of which,* Sleepless Nights, *is part of the* New York Review Books Classics *series. The woman carrying Robert Lowell's child was his third wife, Lady Caroline Blackwood, a journalist and writer.*

. . .

September 25
New York

Dear James-O,
This is to assure you that your play has not yet arrived and to suggest that if you have not already sent it, you use my address for October . . .

I am eager to see it and shall not delay acknowledging its receipt and spelling out its glories in my headiest prose.

I am off next week in a borrowed car for 6 monastic weeks. Mss., notebooks, dictionaries, gluepot, scissors, typewriter, several colors of ink, all the impedimenta of a demented medieval scribe. Pray for me, the Footnote King.

Manhattan gossip: Robt. Lowell is about to become (or already has become) a father—by way of a 45-year-old lady formerly married to Lucien Freud and a poet whose name I always forget. He—Lowell, known since prep-school days as "Cal," for Caligula—is publishing the anguished letters of his second wife, Elizabeth Hardwick, with his commentary: in a private edition of course, which he'll hand out to friends. *Joli*, huh?

Contracts are being drawn up for me to edit three volumes of G. Wescott's journals, beginning next year. *Son coeur mis a nu*, more or less. "It will be an age of journals," said Emerson, one hundred years ago.

I've been working hard (thought not very fruitfully); not even any movies. A tiresome dinner with Ned Rorem this week, at which we battled over Leonard Bernstein, whom I called "the Eric Segal of music." Ned worships *Stardom* and *Time*-mag-spreads above all, but he tried to defend B. as having changed the "face of American musical comedy"!! You see how much better it is to live in Colorado? Last night two old friends of mine arrived from Vienna by way of a summer of Portugal and early September in Paris to enter some sort of Chilean "guru" academy which is run on one entire floor of the Essex House. Their "course" will take three austere months and include yoga, tarot, astrology and other ways and means.

October 7
Aspen

Dear Robert,

Robert, your beautiful book arrived today, I'm reading it, I love to hear you talk, "months with three syllables," "a look of knowing, reproof, and forgiveness." I'm only at the beginning. I see it's about James Agee (yes?) and Becki. It sounds so much like you it's as if you were here. Did you really hang out in all those bars, even then? Thank you for the book. I'll write again in a few days when I've finished it. Of course, I'll never finish it, that is to say, know everything behind it. Do you know the quote of Gide's about "Write this book as if it were your last . . . " I wanted to send it to you to have while you were writing. The summer is standing with its face turned to us for one, last look. I think I'm supposed to hear from the American Place Theatre today. I miss you.

Strength,

J.

Did I ever send you the article about the German critic Benjamin, whose vision was to write in footnotes? Do you know this?

. . .

Elaine Dundy was a writer, best known for her novel The Dud Avocado. *The French writer Jules Renard was a member of the Académie Goncourt. His journals are his only major work available in English.*

. . .

October 10
Peterborough, NH

Dear Jim,

About five o'clock one morning last week, a fox attacked a police dog belonging to the man who directs the Colony. The dog killed the fox, naturally, and as a precaution the fox's head was removed and sent to a laboratory in Concord. It turned out to be rabid, and now the local game warden has authorized the shooting of any animal, tame or wild, that appears to behave oddly. He may even organize a posse to move through the neighboring woods, annihilating every squirrel, rabbit, raccoon, etc. in sight. And meantime little children daren't play Indian.

I have a cabin about half a mile from the road, surrounded by hemlocks and birch, with a sort of corridor beyond my front windows through which I can see Monadnock Mountain. The air is very quiet and very clean. Today it's raining, but softly, a fine mesh when you walk through it, but heavy enough to crepitate audibly on the roof. Alas, my fireplace has been sealed for the winter and I am warmed by a kerosene space heater (most nights I wake up at least once, wondering if the place is on fire and my dozens of journals and bails of mss. are gone). The water is turned off, too, and I have five sturdy pails of water for the john. I live and eat at the main colony hall, and come out here with a thermos about eight. My lunch basket is delivered at eleven thirty and I close up shop about three. One lovely afternoon last week I drove over to Jaffrey Center and paid homage to the grave of Willa Cather. But usually I nap, shave, read [Jules] Renard and mix myself a massive martini (6 parts Tanqueray gin, 0.1 part Noilly Prat, and a shard of lemon rind). Dinner's at 6:30, with occasional gatherings before. Last night it was *chez* Louise Varese, the widow of the composer and translator of Rimbaud, Stendahl, Baudelaire, Simenon. In the evening I tend to go to bed very early, or drive to a movie with Elaine Dundy, ex-wife of Kenneth Tynan and quondam girl-friend of my great hero, Cyril Connolly. She's the liveliest of the guests, most of whom are honest hacks but fairly square in temperament and rather local in their cultivation. But there is one nearly nubile girl whose complexion is ravishing, and of course the autumn leaves have begun to turn (it's a late fall here—no frost yet).

Thank you for your dear letter. I think the essay on Walter Benjamin was by Theodor Adorno, and it wasn't footnotes: he dreamed of composing a book entirely of quotations. I love Benjamin, the little I know of him. He translated Proust into German and killed himself trying to escape the Nazis on the French-Spanish border. I once wrote an essay called "In Praise of Boredom" with a beautiful quote from B., something about "Boredom is the dreambird that hatches the egg of experience." But that's not quite right.

Jim, I am very anxious about the ms. of your play. It had not arrived by October 1st, when I left. Did you really mail it? Becki will forward it, of course. But meantime what are we to make of the post?

The first few days here were very self-conscious—as to working, I mean. But now I seem to be into my morass. Two or three times I've uttered a yip of joy. On the other hand, one day was desperate: my stomach was so distended with nervous gas by 2 o'clock that I had to take off my pants.

October 22
Peterborough, NH

Dear Jim,
The play came this morning, and as evidence, I submit the enclosed portion of the envelope. Postmarked Aspen, Sept. 10, it must have travelled west, all the way around the globe, and by slow freighter, to reach its next postmark at Peterborough, Oct. 20. *Drôle de P.O.*

The play excites me chiefly because it represents (for me) new territory on the Salter continent. I have known the novelist and short story writer and filmmaker and they have all been relatively naturalistic. Meditative and poetic, but real, historical, documentary in their substance. *The Death Star* is all poetic. The situation and characters are emblematic, all seen from a high, unintimate altitude; like heraldry or geodesic survey maps. It's strange, cold, lucid, memorable, generic. There is one line I have already borrowed for a footnote: "Whatever you do without, you are the richer for . . . "

I should think it would build powerfully and austerely in a stage performance. It leaves a complex but single impression, like a giant footprint or maple leaf. Have you heard from the American Place people yet?

If I sound numb it's because I'm exhausted. My book has just undergone another shake-down and now seems to be going to end up 36 short parts and an envoi. I have two brimming waste baskets.

I have not known such an autumn for 15 years: blue and gold and a dozen shades of red; epiphanic starlight at night; high tranquil days, serene, halcyon, sovereign, cloudless. I feel like a Mohawk in 1771. I have met a man who supplies people with wood. Thanks to the death of the elm trees, he takes down 180 a year, some 4 feet in diameter. Did you know that black birch tastes like spearmint when newly cut? The paths and workroads here are ankle deep in maple leaves, birch, oak. Sometimes I can't help feeling like Edna Millay: "Prithee, let no leaf fall . . . "

It's 4 o'clock. I'm going to the library to hear *Wozyck*, or the first act at least; then shave and mix martinis for Elaine Dundy. After dinner a movie, something awful, probably that abomination of Ken Russell's based on Aldous Huxley's *Devils of Loudon*.

. . .

Joseph Papp was a theatre director and producer. Among his accomplishments was the founding of the New York Shakespeare Festival in the 1950s.

. . .

October 26
Aspen

Dear Robert,
Heroes and Orators. I finished reading it yesterday. Not that I haven't been reading it steadily, but you see why I could never be a reviewer. The first thing I think is how far, how very far that is behind you now though I see you with absolute clarity in the writing and even see you sitting, writing. It made me think a bit of *Walliwaw* and also *This Side of Paradise* because of its youth, its vulnerability, its attempts to be whole in ways which are foreign somehow to the writer. And, my God, I'm surprised you have a liver after those years. No wonder your hand trembles slightly. You are a beautiful writer, Robert, and a saintly one. Of course, this was a youthful book. You had not yet found the stream-bed that runs from within to the page. You were admiring things that you do not truly admire, that merely possess the power to disturb you. And you were only beginning to understand how to focus the enormous forces, the knowledge, and the anti-knowledge, within you.

You must write as if it were a letter to someone you love, well, I know you do that, do you? You must write without an audience, without thought of being read, except occasionally, perhaps, there leaks through—one cannot prevent it—a piece of the dream that you are, as Connolly says, writing a masterpiece.

Well, you are making martinis for Elaine Dundy—I know Elaine, I envy her at this moment, embrace her knees for me—and I am carrying oats down to the pony who has a coat already thick as a cat's. The light is where you are, Robert.

As to the play, I see you dozed through the entire first act, as is your custom. The American Place Theatre finally turned it down saying that "the largeness of the subject overwhelmed the dramatic possibilities." It's gone to yr. friend, Jos. Papp. The only thing that encourages me is that your enthusiasm has always directed itself to those things that never found an audience, so perhaps now . . .

I drove to Crested Butte, which is about forty miles from here as the crow flies but a three hour drive over the passes. It's a beautiful, abandoned coal-mining town now being made into a "family" ski resort. Sad to see the melancholy store fronts of the '90s becoming boutiques and cute restaurants and the breathtaking meadows now filled with dry grass and a holy silence, staked off for condominiums and ranchettes. There's a mountain called Gothic Mountain nearby and Crested Butte is the one dominating the town—it's stark as the Eiger.

Don't lose your courage. Finish this book. Believe in it.

It's snowing. I am jealous of you.

November 1
Aspen

Dear Robert,

I am happy, I'm reading Violette Leduc, why does this crazy woman move me so? It's her new book, *Mad in Pursuit*. If you haven't read it, Roger will send you one. It has the most wonderful effect on me: it makes me want to write. An English producer with Japanese money (and only incidentally, a Persian wife) likes *To Warsaw*, the first person to respond since 1957. Anyway, his associates, damn them already, are now reading it in England and he will return to New York on November 15 with The Decision. I don't care. I would rather lope in the woods like a worm-raddled wolf, occasionally sleeping where it's warm. My hero is Jos. Papp. My whole world depends upon him. How else can I be assumed into heaven? Somebody nice has borrowed your book, you have two readers here. Mark it on your map.

November 13
New York

Dear James,
I'm just back from a week at Hay-meadows, the New Jersey estate of the Wescott clan, where I spent 10 hours a day filtering through thousands and thousands of pages of mss., journalia, letters, orts, etc. My big-brother-maître Glenway has lived a strange, glamorous life which he has annotated on the run, and our friend Roger Straus, Jr. has now commissioned me to "edit" three volumes of a diary. It will be a *journal composé*, i.e., a seeming diary, made up of bits of colored glass snipped out of the above masses of typescript and holograph. It must be ready by April and of course it's feeding me this winter. It's over my shoulder, half-bewitched, half-indignant at half a century of his own goings-on. He keeps wanting to re-write! It's like walking for days along the English coast after the wreck of the Armada. The beach is strewn. You keep running back and forth. Everything glitters, even the eyes of dead men.

I can hardly remember October, when I was running up and down my own coastline.

As for Mlle Leduc (who appears in the Wescott diary): I have not only read *Mad in Pursuit* (*Folie en Tête*) but I wrote the blurb (for $75) one desperate day last year when I happened to be in the FS&G office. The editor in charge was too lazy to write it himself and I was too poor to refuse his check. Mlle Leduc is a horror, but I respect her shamelessness. Reading her is a little like watching a snake-swallower. But the book is immortal, for me, if only because it records what that awful Establishment man Paul Valéry said about *Notre Dame des Fleurs*. And before *Esquire* took him up, Genet had a certain real phosphorescence.

I'll pray to my guardian angel about your Papp; and that Japanese wife. (Can't you seduce her somehow? Fucking someone is the only way to expedite matters in this harsh world, I'm sure) . . .

Elaine Dundy told me you were the most adamant wolf she had ever met. Shameless was her word, I think. Aren't you proud of your legend?

. . .

Salter mentions Mabel Dodge in his November 21 letter, an apparent reference to Mabel Dodge Luhan. She was a patron of the arts in America, the Taos art colony in particular. Today the Mabel Dodge Luhan House in Taos offers workshops for artists in various disciplines.

. . .

November 21
Aspen

Dear Robert,

For the moment I'm through playing poker with my children, aged nine, my corgi is lying bellied down in the new sun and snow, and a blessed silence is over everything—people are in church, yes, they do that here, it's one reason (the silence) we must not turn our backs upon religion.

Elaine Dundy is hysterical. I have never been closer to her than one might be in a queue for the Long Island Railroad, she has been slightly closer than that to me, barely. This wicked reputation is largely based upon my silence and certain key pieces of gossip, I was about to say ass but one must not be continually frivolous.

You never said anything about your book. Have all my prayers and emanations during the MacDowell period been in vain? Do you write well when you're drinking or do you have to be pure, concentrating, and in cold possession? This coming—Thanksgiving—week, I'm going to do the extended outline for my book [eventually to become *Light Years*], I already have one twenty pages long plus fifty pages of microscopic notes, but now I must combine and improve these. I love this book. I'm writing it for myself and an audience composed of me's. I expect nothing of it except the refusal of certain eminent writers to endorse it. It's going to have many beautiful jumps, *sauts*, perhaps it will be a ballet. If I can finish it by summer, perhaps it will be done by the time Joseph Papp finally reads my play . . . It's been there five weeks, lying around like any bill, I suppose, not even an inkling from a reader of its reception. I've already decided that for the next round I'm submitting it to three places simultaneously, to hell with the customary. I want my rejections in bunches so I don't care so much about them . . .

I sent "Via Negativa" to Lytle at *The Sewanee Review*. I said you had encouraged me to do it, but otherwise you are blameless. Did I tell you about going to Taos to see Dennis Hopper? In Mabel Dodge's house, which is now his. To work.

. . .

The line that opens Phelps's December 1 letter appears to be from Salter's application to the Guggenheim Foundation. The book of Horst photographs Phelps refers to is Salute to the Thirties. *It is currently out of print.*

. . .

December 1
New York

Dear Jim,

" . . . for if it is to be outrageous and dense it must proceed from the commonplace . . . "

I must get this into a footnote in my memoir. *Echt* Salter. If I had Guggenheims to give, you'd have one for that sentence alone. As it is, I've written an ardent, high-minded page and sent it off . . .

I think I am at some sort of crossroads. I need to fall in love, or be persecuted, or otherwise galvanized. I feel tepid. I have stopped taking Dexedrine and I miss it. Like having one's wings clipped.

If you can afford it, buy Horst's book of thirties photographs (Viking, $17). It has some extraordinary faces, with a marvelous foreword by

Flanner. My son is working for an architect in Boston, and my daughter-in-law has 8 piano students. They bake their own bread and are happy. I spend two or three hours every afternoon back in 1937-38-39 with Mr. Glenway Wescott's photostated diary pages. "There are more things in Heaven & Earth, Horatio, Than are dream't of in your philosophy."

. . .

David Puttnam—Lord David Puttnam, to accord him due respect—made a career in film and one in politics as well. He is a member of Britain's Labour Party and has been elected to the House of Lords.

. . .

December 12
Aspen

Dear Robert,
I like the physical life here. Of course, there is no intellectual life. Bitter cold today. I sat by the fire in the morning and read *The Master Builder*. Why am I writing about myself all the time? Then again, who else do I know?

I am hard at work, hard for me, that is. I won't have finished my book before I receive the Guggenheim rejection, but I'll be well along with it. I'm putting everything in it. If I could slip off my life like a snakeskin and grind it up and sprinkle that too, I would. Some things in it I love as one loves a woman. I lie in bed with them at night, with the thought of them. I've talked to no one about it, absolutely no one. I have two hundred pages of notes plus many scraps of paper. I want this book to be a failure, then I can go right on living as I am. Of course, a failure that frightens people, writers, that is. I want them to think: . . . If he ever gets loose . . . Success would ruin me. I'm a century plant, I'm only going to bloom once, and I hope that's the year I die.

To California on my credit card to see an English producer very interested in *To Warsaw*. David Puttnam. I don't know what I expected, a somewhat slick man of forty-three. Instead I met a kid in Levi's and a Levi jacket, Christlike beard and hair, not much over thirty, who was deeply involved in a film of Speer's book about Germany (Donald Pleasence as Hitler). As I did expect, however, we said very little about *Warsaw*, perhaps three paragraphs towards the end of the evening. With us was his "researcher," a girl in Levi's too who was absolutely "mad about films." I must say, she did make it a pleasant dinner . . .

I'm glad to hear you don't have Parkinson's, I want you to be my literary executor, it's not a big job, you can do it in a couple of weeks.

December 15
New York

Dear Aspen,
What do you mean, I "don't have Parkinson's"? Tuesday I had a cortisone injection in my right arm, and only last night (7pm) I began taking something called Adolpo (as in El Topo), which is medical science's newest "cure" for the shakes. It's supposed to be a ruthless aphrodisiac as well, so I expect my ejaculation rate (circa 18 per week) to skyrocket.

And thank you, but no, I decline to be anyone else's lit. exec. Wescott has, so to speak, filled my cup to brimming with that privilege. Try Elaine Dundy—who, incidentally, was removed from the MacD Colony. When she hadn't turned up for dinner in four successive days, the director looked in her room and found her soused. Which also explained where everyone else's liquor had gone. *Poverina*.

"Success would ruin me." But if success doesn't, something else will. Why not give success a chance? As Dr. Johnson said, a genius is never destroyed by anything but himself. You're the strong, dark, silent type. Be unafraid . . .

My novel lies comatose and waiting for lots of suturing. I haven't touched it since my 31 days in New Hampshire. Since coming back I have been awash in 1625 pp. of Someone Else's Ego; and 38 pp. of an unfinished story of my own, about being blown for the first time when I was 18. It's called "Sixteen Thousand Words in Praise of Billy Beaularis." Sort of a memo to my happily married son, who is working for an architect in Boston this month.

1972

Yours in Exile, Yours in Bliss

Salter began work on Light Years *in 1972, and though he devoted some time to film work, the year was given mostly to the novel and efforts to place* The Death Star *with a theatre. Phelps, on the other hand, suffered through a year of doubts. In one letter that year he wrote, "As it is, for 20 years, I have only scrounged at making a living: a low standard of survival and hundreds of articles, reviews, flower arrangements of other people's prose, etc. Not a good form of hell at all." Perhaps worst of all, his trembling hand remained a problem.*

. . .

> *The reports of Peter O'Toole's drinking in Salter's January 13 letter were apparently not exaggerated. A recent book by Robert Sellers entitled* Hellraisers: The Life and Inebriated Times of Richard Burton, Richard Harris, Peter O'Toole and Oliver Reed, *speaks to O'Toole's excesses.*

. . .

January 13
Aspen

Dear Robert,

A great blizzard today, the snow unusually fine. I rose this morning and braved it with my dog, snow freezing to his whiskers, then sat by the fire and read Violette Leduc on Cocteau and Jean Genet. I love her, she's so agonized, so hysterical, so hopeless, so clear. I began the writing of my own book on the 11th. Of course, I can't believe in it yet, I've written so little. I expect my devotion to grow. It looks as if it will be long, long for me. I have 65 pages of outline, not to mention 150, at least, of notes. All this to be entitled to write a single paragraph, the last paragraph of the book.

The good news is I believe I've sold my house (in Nyack) and hope to close in February. If that's the case, I'll be coming to New York. I have all the furniture and books to pack or throw away. I think there are two volumes of Mlle. de Beauvoir's autobiography there which I'd like to read (Violette talks about her so much, reveres her). The Rosenthals are well settled-in, at last, in Rome. They had the small chalet of a friend for Christmas (about three weeks) in a Swiss village called Chandolin, fifty inhabitants, my daughter tells me, and the cows are kept in the houses. I loved the description. Anything would be better than this, where the news announcer calls Mme. Gandhi "Gahandi" and spells out the words—they are numerous—he can't pronounce. When my Guggenheim comes—that's all right, I like to think of it that way—I'm sailing to Europe tourist class on the *Elizabeth II* and visiting them. I've instructed her to begin reading the Pavese short stories in that elegant, paper edition of Einaudi, I doubt she will. She's a vegetarian, a gentle heart, she longs to move into some inarticulate young man's cabin, weave and read a little Hindu mythology. Meanwhile, she's having dinner with the Peter O'Tooles (they—he is in the film) and reporting his habits, jokes, and the amount of pear brandy he puts away (a bottle at a sitting). His favorite expression: Jesus fucking Christ and Holy shitting Mary.

It's awful that so many books in the past year or two have a present participle in the title: *Making Do*, *Taking Off*, *Getting High*, *Coming On*, etc. My own title predates these, I've had it for five years, dare I use it now? *Entering Death*.

. . .

Baron Guy de Rothschild was a French banker. Apart from his prominence in the financial world, he was noted for his family's wine (Château Lafite Rothschild).

. . .

January 18
New York

I don't know what "tendonitis" is, but Tony Randall appears to have had it since last July—acute pain in the right arm—he can no longer even shake hands. I learned this as I was falling asleep last night (Becki drowsing herself on the TV, with the eye aimed away from my bed, so I could only hear, not see); and I woke up at seven this morning convinced that, after all, I had Mr. Randall's affliction, not mere "bursitis" or solemn Hopkinson's disease. So I shuffled glumly out to my coffee, remembering lines from Auden*,

*And out of the open sky
The pantocratic riddle breaks—
"Who are you and why?"

rubbing my eyes, tripping over the cat. On the kitchen table I found an album of Canaletto's Venetian paintings and after an hour's wandering through his loggias and up and down his staircases, I felt quickened—not really alive, but less dormant, less scaly. I dressed, pausing between socks to dote on Canaletto's picture of the Santo Giovanni e Paulo church where my beloved Stravinsky's funeral was held last April; then came on down to my crib and the morning mail to find your blizzard bulletin. It was to Canaletto what Houseman's malt was to Milton*,

*Malt does more than Milton can
To justify God's ways toward man.

thank you. I have since been to the bank, made an appointment with the barber downstairs, and am prepared to make use of this 18th day of the new year by resuming work on my book. As you can see for yourself, I have even changed typewriter ribbons in mid-page, ever a sound augury.

In my past several weeks' mute desperation, I have been reading Ungaretti's poems. How did I ever get the idea that I was a novelist? I am a "lyric leak" (Henry James). I love Ungaretti, as I love his friend Apollinaire, because they both wrote SHORT verbals. One of the reasons

I love *A Sport* so much is because it is made up of, say, eighty, shortish poems. And speaking of that book, I must invent some new lines about it. For at least the tenth time, I heard myself (yesterday evening, in a bar on Park Avenue South, with David MacDowell, my first editor) repeating my set speech about it being "the most original American novel published in the sixties."

Tell your daughter that I am moving to Rome on October 6th for three or four months, or perhaps life. I am not an "inarticulate young man"—God pity me, but perhaps she could do a little weaving while I watched and read bits of Pavese to her in baby-pidgin Italian.*

*E.G., "*Il vero vizio era questo piacere*
di starmene sola"—or "*Aver dei soldi*
vuol dire poterti isolare . . . " both from
Tra Donne Sole, one of the books
which never fails to nourish me.

Incidentally, are Peter O'Toole's eyes as bloodshot in real life as they are on the screen? Perhaps like Elizabeth Taylor's ravishing mole, they are only another triumph of the makeup department.*

*A canard, surely.

I agree about the recent abuse of present participles. I have an unfinished novel (1959–1960) called *Shifting Down*; and the original title of Tennessee Wm's *Orpheus Descending* was *Orpheus Going Down*. But back in the fifties, his producer wouldn't permit it. Imagine. I also wrote a story called "Entering Aries," but Lousie Bogan, to whom it was dedicated, lost the only ms. or at least never returned it, and then died. *Entering Death* is imposing, I think, and not unmemorable.

If you are coming east in February, please let me know just when, so I can take you up to Melville's grave, or down to a marvelous herb shop near City Hall. And we'll have some clams at Paddy's: it looks as bleak as a Hopper painting, but the seafood is the freshest in NY.

My son is working as a gardener, very happy, and his wife has nine piano pupils. They are planning to live in Salzburg next summer, to hear Mozart all day and read German. Glenway Wescott comes back from Christmas with the Baron de Rothschild today, and I only have two years of his diary pasted up. I lost my gloves, but I'm keeping an eye on the apartment next door while its owners are skiing, so I've borrowed a pair. No use wasting money on a pair of my own.

January 21
Aspen

Dear Robert,
Yes, hard at work, the end of the day, my eyes are tired, as burning as if I were driving to Nyack from a day in New York. My mind has slipped and fallen, I've done nothing today, three or four pages, I can't believe there's a sentence worth saving in them, I don't even read them, I'm pushing on, the winter's half over, I must be there this spring . . .

I'd like to go to Amagansett, Sagaponack, or anywhere near this summer, myself, some musician's or painter's simple house, alone, and work. I'd bring my dog, that's all.

I went to see *Women in Love* for the third time. All the blemishes are showing in it for me now, but it has some wonderful performances and of course, Lawrence sings to me. As I left, I was behind two young women, twenty perhaps, winter guests, Aspen is filled with them.

"Well, I didn't get much out of that," one said, "did you?"

"I thought it was fucking boring."

"Yeah maybe it was good in its time."

"Um."

Vladimir Nabokov is coming here this summer. Bellow will be back. I dread it all, I dread the cries of children in the street. Well, I'll be rich. The Guggenheim money, my house money, plus a five hundred dollar advance on my book—would Roger [Straus, of Farrar, Straus & Giroux] do that?—I am going to purchase . . .

Silence

Saturday morning. The weather saves us and the weather kills us. Today is grey, inert, a little too warm. How awful it is to wake up in the same old life. I was encouraged by your reaction to my title. I haven't legitimized it but I do put it on the notebook covers. The trouble is, it's a title that the book, a book, must struggle against, must win you in spite of. I'm so pleased to be writing about America, at last, anyway life in America. I miss you deeply. I am a literary ragpicker, I know something of this and that but my knowledge is not coherent, it does not spread over everything. I'm going to list all the writers I've never read, it will be a roll call of the great. You are far more educated. Why don't I listen to you more instead of talking? I'm afraid to, I suppose. I would sit there knowing less and less, or realizing I know less and less. People here are so stupid, so thin, and they are not even the struggling stupid. They have their wit and they have their desires. I learned at dinner last night that a very devoted couple, a couple whose house is redolent of conjugal life, who devote themselves to two children, a rich couple, of course: he lives four days at home and three days with another woman. I love the wife's name, Meta, she's very good-looking, she has a slight lisp. The second one is a legendary creature from Oklahoma, I've never seen her, there are dozens of stories, her name is Garvine(!)

As Simone de Beauvoir said constantly: Work!

February 3
Aspen

Dear Robert,
I don't dare tell you what I'm doing. I don't believe in what I'm doing, I'm merely pledged to it, like marriage, I'm driving on through the winter as if on snow shoes.

A long and very analytical letter from Andrew Lytle. He asks me to tell you to get that review in. He says I have committed a violation by shifting the point of view in the story and that he has found when an author violates the point of view "he is backing off from the crisis of his action." He says the "enveloping action of any kind of universal or archetypal truth is obscure" in the story. This and more. It's true, most stories do have a single point of view: that of the writer. In my opinion, he is free to go wherever he likes, so long as he compels or, at least, interests. The rest is merely dry theory and one writes with one's instincts.

Nevertheless, I appreciated the length and thoughtfulness of the letter which invites me to send something else. I don't like magazines that reject me, I don't like those that accept me. My tea is cold. My life is cooling.

. . .

Natalie Clifford Barney was the longtime host of a literary salon in Paris. She was also openly lesbian. Paul Horgan's notable works deal with the American Southwest. He was twice awarded the Pulitzer Prize for Nonfiction. For this reason, Phelps seems to have found his writing about Igor Stravinsky unusual. Sir Cecil Beaton was a photographer, but he also earned three Academy Awards, one for his costume design on Gigi *(1958) and two—for set decoration and costume design—on* My Fair Lady *(1964).*

. . .

February 8
New York

Mon frère,
Which story did you send Andrew? The one that eager little Cynthia Buchanan typed for you last year? (And have you seen her busty photograph in the book reviews? Apparently Barbra Streisand's agent bought, or optioned, the novel,—hence these full-page ads.) . . .

My wellshaft is so cold this morning that I can see my breath. I am typing with three fingers and not thinking of what I'm saying. This evening I go to the opening of something called "1922—A Vintage Year" at the Berg Collection—the rare book room of the NY Public Library. It seems the show is based on the *Literary Life* chapter for that year. I want to see the ms. books of Va. Woolf's diaries, so I'm out to get into the good graces of the director, a lady called Lola Szladits.

Last night I went around to the Presbyterian Chapel at Fifth Ave. and 11th Street to say good-bye to Marianne Moore, a grand lady, and a sterling example of sticking to one's own idiosyncrasies-madness-vision for 84+ years. I remember once calling for her, to escort her to some party. It was a ghastly hot July afternoon, and she met me at the door in her underskirt. After showing me a photograph of T. S. Eliot *jeune*, she asked me to help her with her dress. It was hanging in the shower, and she explained that this was the best way to "press" a velvet dress: fill the shower with steam, then hang the dress in the fog for an hour. She was 81 that year and I had the honor of doing up the snaps at her back. Before we left she insisted I take five dollars (in one-dollar bills) for the cabs and when I indignantly left them on her desk she nattered at me all the way down in the elevator. Someone else told me she always kept a bowl of subway tokens and when a guest left, she handed him the fare home. Her great lifetime muse and companion was her mother. (There is a magnificent photo of the two of them by Cecil Beaton). When the mother died, Monroe Wheeler escorted Marianne to Gettysburg to bury the ashes. In the car he held the urn in his lap, and along the way they stopped at a snake farm.

And Natalie Clifford Barney took off last week too; at 96. A week earlier I had received a book from her and was writing to thank her the morning I heard about her death. She was born in Dayton, Ohio, near my own place of coming forth, but she had money and escaped early and on her own terms. She wrote aphorisms in French which are first rate. It was she who said, "Indiscretion is the privilege of tact."

I think of you every day, sipping your tea at the desk I glimpsed in Case's movie. *Downhill Racer* was on TV a couple of weeks ago and your peculiar cachet is there in spite of the stars and snappy direction. (The scene in the men's room when Redford looks at himself in the mirror, waiting to go back to his table and "encounter" the girl; the scenes with the father.)

I'm reading two more books about Stravinsky—[Robert] Craft's summation, and a memoir by—of all people—Paul Horgan. Marvelous Igor: as a man and as a maker he is for me the most valuable and nourishing creator of our century. I love his music—every bar of it, as passionate and impeccably wrought as Bach's.

If you are ploughing ahead on "snowshoes," I'm standing still, in stocking-feet and half-frozen. I must be passing through some sort of climacteric (as Glenway says, the old age of youth, or the youth of old age). I have never worked so desperately hard to achieve so miserably little. My hand continues to shake. It's all neurotic, I'm sure. *Il faut payer*—but in my case, it's mostly for sins of omission, I'm afraid.

And Auden is leaving America, re-patriating to become its resident grand, dirty old man. I love him too.

. . .

Mawrdew Czgowchwz *is a novel by James McCourt. Ted Solotaroff was the founder and editor of* The New American Review, *a literary magazine which published work by Philip Roth, Donald Barthelme, and countless others. Jules Irving co-founded the San Francisco Actors' Workshop with Herb Blau. He also served as artistic director of the Lincoln Center Repertory Theater and experimental forum.*

. . .

March 6 or 7
Aspen

Dear Robert,
Having saluted you, it has become March 9th.

The winter is in panic here, the snow running from the mountains in rivulets. I hate the change of seasons, my blood becomes confused.

They are trying to persuade my daughter to remain another year in Rome, but life is more *dolce* here, I think she thinks, and I expect her home. Meanwhile, I am daily going to the post office expecting my rejection by the Guggenheims, but nothing yet.

I am finishing *Mad in Pursuit*. It ends in confusion and is not the book *La Batarde* was but there are things in it that . . . "Recently I pressed Beckett's Malloy against one cheek, then against the other . . . A great writer is a great brother, he just falls into your life, it is stronger than any bond of blood."

I'm on page 115 (of my own book). I hardly remember what is behind me. It's like a densely enacted journey during which you've made no notes. When I'm finished with this first, tedious working-out, in the summer, I'm going to look at it like a ruined garden, I hope I will, with dimensions that please, lovely corners, walls, and weeds, weeds everywhere . . .

Did you read *Mawrdew Czgowchwz* in your friend Ted Solotaroff's review? I'm a fool for listening to talk, falling for it. I picked up that issue (13), my hands were almost trembling, and I found an amusing story clearly descended from Edward Gorey's *La Chauve-Souris Dorée* (that's supposed to be a children's book, if you don't know it, I haven't yet been able to interest any child in it, but I love it, you can read it in ten minutes). Yesterday someone I had to listen to urged me to read *The Day of the Jackal*, marvelous book they said, I was licking my dry lips trying to make my mind wander, you couldn't put it down they said. Well if you read Tolstoy or Proust or Dickens, I said, you will find just the opposite, that you have to put them down.

Which explains why I haven't written lately, I had to put you down. I still expect to be in NY a month from now. I want to sleep in the best theatres. Will you come?

. . .

Maeve Brennan was a writer, perhaps best known for her book In and Out of Never-Never Land.

. . .

April 11
New York

Dear James,
I had forgotten about the Guggenheims (I did not apply this year myself, having (a) nothing to show for several years but journalism and (b) no enthusiastic sponsors). I do remember writing a couple of urgent pages about the *oeuvres complets de* J. Salter, however—did I send you a carbon? Keep trying, as I was once told. No one any good has ever gotten aureoled the first time around. De Kooning was rejected eleven times; Agee nine or ten . . .

As Auden says in one of his titles, "Another time."

Did I tell you about my dinner with Auden—farewell dinner, as he's leaving this week for several decades of his second childhood at Oxford—? He arrived promptly (*chez un ami*) at 7, drank six martinis, most of two bottles of burgundy and at precisely 9:30, leapt up from the table and was gone. He's getting plump so some of those fantastic wrinkles are filling out, making him look younger than he did 10 or 20 years ago. Almost his first words on arriving were "Of course T. S. Eliot was 40% queer"—this apropos of Valéry, whose picture Auden keeps above his desk and who was not a bit queer. And apropos of giving up smoking, he observed that "Of course for a lifetime cock-sucker it's especially hard, but I've promised myself compensations." He, too, loves Trollope (there's a piece on him in the recent *NYer*), but is appalled at Lowell's having privately published his letters from Elizabeth Hardwick. ("I'm afraid I won't be able to speak to Cal any-more.") And so on; genial but somehow "cooled," no longer molten or in ferment. He tends to quote himself—from his own writings, that is—as though all of his tastes and opinions had long since crystallized. A successful but no longer quite interesting child.

Yesterday we had word that the apartment above ours will become available in June. Which will give us some room—the entire floor we now have to become Becki's studio-den-zoo-etc., and a large front room with fireplace to become my *chambre à soi*—finally. With a kitchen, common room and bath at the rear. I can no longer work in this hallway, and I badly need a place where I can see a wide variety of people one-at-a-time, without domesticity or anyone else's ego in sight.

My novel is shelved—or has been since about Christmas. It fell apart—or I did. A climacteric of some sort, of which my trembling right hand is only a tiny symptom. I am editing Wescott's diaries at the moment, and working at an unfinished story (I want to FINISH something). To pay this month's rent I have just done a *Life* squib on Papa Stravinsky. I wish I could write three-line poems.

Asked if he'd miss the cultural life (sic) of New York, Auden said no, because he had never taken part in it. "I read, listen to records, and do crossword puzzles." *Moi aussi*. Rather to my dismay I find that this week I am reading the following: some memoirs of Gertrude Stein's collaborationist friend Bernard Faÿ; Pierre Boulez's *Notes of an Apprenticeship*; a biography by André Billy of Mérimée; [Eugène] Fromentin's *Dominique*; assorted very short stories by Jules Renard; Wescott typescript from 1943–44; and Walter Scott's essay on Samuel Richardson. Not healthy. I wish I were in love, or at least in lust. (Wescott: "Lust is pure, love corrupts.")

Please let me know when you'll be here. I'll save my pocket money and we'll go to a quiet steak house where we can have cold martinis and rare filets mignons and talk until it's late enough for a nightcap brandy at Casey's.

A couple of months ago I ordered a book from Rizzoli. This morning came a notice of its arrival,—and its cost: $85.00 plus city tax! I also had an invitation from "Le Conseiller Culturel" to the French ambassador to a reception for Louise Varese (age 80, widow of the composer, and my 3rd love at the MacDowell Colony last fall—the others were Maeve Brennan, who is currently sweating out a nervous breakdown at the University Hospital here, and your Elaine Dundy, carried off in a closed car sometime in November for a de-hydrating clinic in Massachusetts).

Now I must try to type a page for my story. My right hand is sending me messages. Ach.

. . .

S. N. Behrman was a Broadway playwright, best known for his comedies and, later, his personal writings in The New Yorker. *Ellis Rabb was an actor and director. He appeared in various television series, but the highlight of his career was a Tony Award for his direction of* The Royal Family.

. . .

June 1
Aspen

Dear Robert,

Quiet days in Colorado. We are musing on the idea of a celebration to welcome the daughter back from Rome. She's supposed to arrive in New York via Alitalia on the 10th. After a sketchy tour among various relatives in the east, she should appear here on the 16th, maybe sooner. I expect to find her absolutely unchanged, though she has sworn to me she's reading Pavese. She will find me older, a step nearer the greater world about which we can only speculate.

Becki, I'm having your beautiful pastel sketch framed tomorrow. I'm very fond of it, both for what it is and because you gave it to me. An important turning in my book comes with the gift of a volume about Kandinsky—reading about the lives of others is one of the things that gives us the courage to change our own, the courage to struggle against our own, I suppose.

I've been reading the memoirs of S. N. Behrman in *The New Yorker*. In the beginning of the first installment, he quotes Maugham and Mark Twain as to the impossibility of publishing real journals or even keeping them, perhaps. You might be interested in that. For the rest of it: Endless earnestness, sincerity, and anecdotes of the "now" people of then, especially Jed Harris (will we ever forget his productions of *Love 'Em and Leave 'Em* and *Broadway*?) It's depressing to read minor talents writing about themselves with the conceit that they are as important as anyone. Almost nobody is as important as anyone.

Ellis Rabb—unquestionably you know him, given your devotion to the theatre (Behrman quotes Conrad's literary executor to the effect that Conrad hated the theatre and everything about it)—Ellis Rabb has written that he likes *Death Star*, finds it impressive and arresting and would like to do it at Lincoln Center where he's supposed to direct a play at the Vivian Beaumont next season. He asks we send it to Jules Irving and I am now hoping these two independent but connected interests will push the play into production. I suppose you won't go.

How is your new flat? I never brought you that firewood. Don't worry, you'll have it before winter. I miss you. What news of Wescott?

July 20
New York

Dear Jim,

I owe you three letters but this is none of them,—only a stop-gap, pro-tem, untelegraphed letter in the breech.

I have been happy for weeks, since moving upstairs, where I have a room of my own. I hardly go out. I have cancelled the month in Maine. I don't even like to answer the telephone. For the first time in my life I have a place where my books, mss., *imagi*, totems, and that soft, furtive furry little something I call my psyche can come together. Montaigne: "Miserable, to my mind, is he who has not in his home a place to himself, where he may give all his attention to himself; where he may hide!" I came across this sentence the first week I was here, and I intend to transcribe it over the door. Day after day I simply gloat; browse; read at half a dozen different books; listen to Stravinsky; scribble; nap; wake up and gloat again. How I have ever lived otherwise I can't say.

Of course I am doing no work. One book review last month; paragraphs on my own book; and apart from this, only pasting away at volume two of Glenway Wescott's journal. All this week I have been happily, strangely buried in his A.D. 1949—when among other things, his Italian lover seduced his divorced sister—better than *The Forsyte Saga* by far.

You emerged elegantly and pungently in the film interview [Jim Case's documentary *The Artist in America*]. Becki is in love with you. She woke me up at 5 A.M. one morning to declare you were the only "mensch" we knew. A mixed compliment in my view, but she meant it as extravagant praise.

I'll find a place for you at the end of August; perhaps I'll board you next door in the apartment just sub-let by Maeve Brennan and her three cats. Perhaps I'll put you on the second floor of this bldg with the New York editress whose affair with Clay Felker [founder of *New York Magazine*] is ebbing. Perhaps I'll even buy a folding cot and put you at the other end of my own room. It has no other furniture yet, except a folding chair and bookcases and my desk. But it does have a sturdy air conditioner, thank God, as this is our 9th successive day of hellish heat and non-breathable air. A letter tomorrow.

. . .

The Disintegration of James Cherry *is a play by Jeff Wanshel.*

. . .

August 17 or 18
The Summer is Ended
Aspen

Dear Robt.,
One letter before I sit down to work, I am not quite ready. The morning is always like that, I wake without belief, without interest, without strength. But a few minutes ago, searching for the place to insert an anecdote about marriage I'd heard, a place in my manuscript which is now almost 300 pages, I had a wonderful thing happen to me, I suddenly realized: it's there! I had begun to read and I saw that I liked it, even more, I was completely taken by it, and also, for the first time I caught that faint glimmer that is light at the end of the tunnel. To think that this will be a book, and a book that I am deeply interested in, that comes from the vitals, as Kazantzakis said. Suddenly I am filled with energy.

Lincoln Center, meanwhile, has been writing to me, they like my play, they want to do it. Unfortunately they haven't the money in their budget for anything so big this season. They propose a Monday night reading, with an option to produce it afterwards. They'll pay well: seventy-five dollars. Even Plimpton does better than that. Ellis Rabb wants to direct the reading. There have been only two previous such readings, one of them ending in a production (*The Disintegration of James Cherry*). I've also had a very nice letter from Royal Court, in London. They admire it greatly but with the same problems. It's still under discussion there. They want me to try the National Theatre and the RSC as well. I've written again to Paul Scofield, asking if he's interested in the role of General Stardoy, I stupidly failed to emphasize that when I first sent the play to him, consequently he never read it.

Redford's been here, visiting. What a lovely life success brings. He has a film next month to do, perhaps one in January, and then *Gatsby* in May.

I miss you, I miss hearing from you. What a long, long voyage this all is. Are you still going to Europe? And your right hand, has it decided to obey?

September 5
Aspen

Dear Robert,
I am packing for Rome. Have your plans changed? Are you so *contento* in your new place that a voyage seems a burden? No.

There's a private plane flying to New York on September 17, on which I might catch a ride. I think I'm going to accept the Lincoln Center offer of a reading in the Forum. It would be sometime after January with an option on their part to produce the play thereafter. Nothing better seems in the offing.

Aspen has been like England, rain every day. A small crabapple tree in my garden that was dry and dispirited all summer has suddenly burst into life—no apples but its leaves are shimmering and its trunk gleams.

I'm into the 300s. I love my book and with a curious, blind satisfaction. It's a confident book, selfish and disdaining comparisons. It also has a lot of strength in it, a mature strength I was never ready to give until now. My fear is that it might be too slow and stuffy. It has no bizarre names, no outrageous details. It's like a river, vast, glinting in the light. I want to finish it, I don't want to finish it.

. . .

Pierre Boulez was a French composer and conductor. Lance Reventlow was Cary Grant's stepson, also a race car driver; he died in small plane crash in 1972.

. . .

September 8
New York

Caro Giacomo,
I remember an interview in which Pasolini said he almost never read a book anymore, nor went to a movie, since for the past four or five years his own work had absorbed him completely. What a test. You pass it, headily. I fail, as witness the books—dozens of them—in three languages, on my table. (Including a new one by Pasolini himself, called *Empirisimo Eretico*, which of course I can barely read two consecutive lines of).

In other words, it's been a lost summer. I have not been, strictly speaking, unhappy. And I've rarely left my new *gite*. I've sat here at my desk with my shaky right paw; I've listened to hours of music; I've read *La Fiera Letteraria* and *L'Expresso*, and *Nouvelles Littéraires* and *L'Express*, and the *Observer* and *TLS*; I've read Dryden's translation (wonderful) of Virgil's *Bucolics and Georgics*; I've read Montale and Arbasino and Ungaretti; I'm reading Wm. Jay Smith's new collection of essays and I've tried to read Hortense Calisher's ghastly pair of new books; I've read Henry Miller's pamphlet on the death of Mishima and the 17th volume of Jouhandeau's diary; I'm reading Charles Rosen's book on Haydn and Beethoven and I've finished Boulez's *Notes of an Apprenticeship*; I've even memorized a couple of poems from Auden's *Epistle to a Godson*. I'm composing (not writing) an essay on what happened in 1922 (Gide, at 53, knocked up the teen-aged daughter of his old friend, Madame van Rysselberghe; Va. Woolf had a 7-month nervous breakdown; Valéry went to London and was paid 25 pounds by Lady Rothmere to read his poems in her salon; Dostoievski was 100 years old; etc).

You see? The situation is very grave.

Next door, temporarily nesting in Newell Jenkins' apartment, is Maeve Brennan, almost as paralyzed as I. We have a martini together occasionally and every morning I look in to be sure she's fed her three cats. One day of the week she goes to the hairdresser; another to her Australian analyst; another to her *NYer* office. The rest of the time she paces and chaffs.

But what will you be doing in Rome? You mentioned a script to be Salterized—is that still it? Autumn in Rome!

Pour gagner la vie, I've been scissoring away at Wescott all summer. One of the reasons I'm stalled is doubtless too much intimacy with the obiter scripta of another stalled writer. At the moment, I'm nauseated, but if I'm to get to Paris in November, I must finish the present volume (3!).

What news can I give you? A couple of weeks ago a 17-year-old girl with flax-yellow hair threw herself out of a 14-story window at Fifth and 12th street. The sidewalk is made of very porous cement and her bloodstains are still there, though of course as someone said, time is darkening them. She was a mini-star in a couple of Andy Warhol's films and was high the afternoon she tried to fly. She was carrying a Bible at the time.

A French friend of mine is working as the cameraman on a pornographic film and I spoke to the director (one Victor Milt), thinking it might do me good to get off my tail and observe something and write about it. He was willing—at the same time explaining to me that he was making this film only because it was the only way to get directing experience these days, what with Hollywood shut down, etc.—but *Life*, *Atlantic Monthly*, etc. declined my lance. "Who do you think you are, Norman Mailer?" said Mr. Scherman. And so what might have been the definitive description of cunnilingus missed its big chance.

"I'm into the 300s . . . " Golden words. The book sounds absolute, certain and unafraid. I shall begin to live vicariously in you.

Beware of "private planes." Remember what happened to Lance Reventlow, whom I last (and first) beheld in the spring of 1957, driving a fantastic Maserati at Sebring. I suppose he has been deposited in the family vault in the Bronx's Woodlawn, where Herman Melville abides in a cemetery laid out during the Civil War to accommodate the sudden upswing in funerals.

The 17th? Will you phone and come down? I'll lend you my bed and room. It's noisy, but after your Aspen silences, it should be a curious change. Besides you'll need conditioning for the roar of Rome.

. . .

Edna O'Brien is one of the major Irish writers of the 20th century, the author of A Pagan Place *and a trio of novels (*The Country Girls, The Lonely Girl, *and* The Girls in Their Married Bliss*) collected as* The Country Girls Trilogy.

. . .

November 2
On board an Alitalia jet
Pound is dead
A literary and monetary statement

Dear Rbto.,
Letters of rejection, this is an entire chapter. I had a very nice one from the RSC. The man who wrote it, stunningly, had been "bowled over" by my flying books. So we met. He was Ronald Bryden, ex–book critic for *The Listener* and *The Spectator*, ex–drama critic, now play finder for the Royal Shakespeare Co. Lovely, awkward Englishman. Invited me to send him my next play. It is always one step further, one more year. Meanwhile planes are falling from the sky, trains are crashing, I am en route to Rome to rewrite a film for Chris Mankiewicz. I have character notes written on menus, *Paris Tribunes*, envelopes, I'm willing to bet the film will never be made, but the money is enough for six months.

Dinner last night with Edna O'Brien. And her son. She has a play, drawn from her book *A Pagan Place* which has been in previews and opens tonight. She was nerves, self-involvement, insecurity. She ate everything with her fingers, lamb, clumps of spinach, they didn't even have to wash her fork. She told me about a new story in *The New Yorker* called "Over," 20,000 words, they paid her $2,800, I don't think that's enough. Candida O'Donadio is her agent. Yes, I said, *The New Yorker*, I've heard of it. She was marvelous, she could recite great passages, long pieces of her story, there was one sentence saying something like: I liked your voice and the way you poured things and your fingering. Her editor, Rachel ________, in the vastly inquisitorial galleys, wrote "Mr. Shawn thinks this is a little too strong for us." So Edna changed it to "and your fucking." I didn't have enough money to pay for dinner.

We land in Rome in three-quarters of an hour. I don't think I'll be able to stop in New York on the way home, will have to go straight through.

November 7
Aboard TWA flight

Dear Robert,
I've been four days in Rome and then flying back on one of those enormous jumbos that have set ocean crossing back to where it was in the 1950s. Every seat filled, children crying, an illiterate passenger agent announcing the start of the film, the sale of drinks, etc. I reached New York last night after six, had a drink, fell over and am off this morning for Denver, I must get home to vote and help stem the Nixon tide. So I won't see you this time, much to my regret. I've had the wonderful news that Jules Irving has parted with Lincoln Center and the entire Forum theatre program including my play may be cancelled. With luck like this there's no need for talent, it is, in fact, wasted.

I took a six-week film assignment to see me through the winter and probably the spring. I'll have the money to finish my book. Presumably then I'll get an advance and so on in a continuing cycle of work. I want to do another play. The RSC play finder asked me to meet him in London which I, dragging my feet like a hermit genius, did swiftly. We had tea in a hotel. Ezra Pound has just died. The RSC man, by a wild and felicitous coincidence, had read those old flying books of mine and admired them greatly. However, you understand, all this against a background of their turning down this play. It is all two steps forward, three steps back.

We are taxiing out. There are ten people aboard, so blessedly empty that the captain had me onto the flight deck to read the Denver and Grand Junction weather to me.

Go to Venice. Take gloves and warm clothes. It will be beautiful, it will be cold. I, myself, am supposed to be back in Rome on December 11 or 12, my work done, and spend a week or two there attendant to the whims of my employers. Then the winter to myself. How good a little money in your pocket makes you feel.

Your life is the correct life. One of the clues to it is your getting rid of all books that are unworthy (except certain personal favorites, of course: Gore Vidal, Mailer . . .). Your desk is the desk of a man who cannot be bought. Your icy gin in the late afternoon is as beautiful to me as Hemingway's days in Paris . . .

And now, all you bills and tradesmen, beware!

. . .

*The writer Muriel Spark (*The Prime of Miss Jean Brody*) is mentioned in the following letter, as well as Phelps's misgivings about the path he has taken as a writer. Hélène Jourdan-Morhange was a violinist. She was married to the painter Jacques Jourdan and was well-acquainted with the composer Maurice Ravel, who once proposed marriage to her, an offer she refused.*

. . .

November 10
New York

Dear James,

Your letters are part of my gospel. It seems to me it was only Monday morning that I read your Rome letter as I walked across Union Square (and under the equestrian statue of Geo. Washington which Henry James described in *An International Episode*) on my way to cover an overdraft at the bank. I'll never forget Miss O'Brien's way with spinach. (And as for paying the check, I once had a similar dinner with Muriel Spark, who told me after at least every other mouthful that her tax accountant advised, indeed, insisted, she be the host). And now, Friday morning, again on my way to the bank, I find you're back in Aspen.

You are wrong about my "life." It would be correct only if it were productive of worthy books. As it is, for 20 years, I have only scrounged at making a living: a low standard of survival and hundreds of articles, reviews, flower arrangements of other people's prose, etc. Not a good form of hell at all. This has become terribly clear to me in the past 6 weeks when I have been going through sheaves of old printed matter with a view to making our publisher a book called *Following*. I have been appalled by the waste, the thousands and thousands of irretrievable words on which nevertheless I worked long and hard and sometimes until 5 A.M. No. Somewhere I took a wrong turning. I should not have tried to earn my living with my typewriter. I should have become a surveyor, or an airline ticket salesman, or a cat burglar. As it is, I am far far beyond the point of no return and such powers as I once counted on—the ability to write to order and out of my own battiness, so to speak—are suddenly gone. All this week I have tried to write two thousand words on Don Quixote for *Playbill* (sic). The pay is honest: $300. The assignment would have thrilled me ten years, five years ago. But today I am sterile, mute, empty-headed, helplessly, obstinately uninspired. Even Dexedrine is no help. And at times my poor right hand shakes so violently I have to laugh. The message is explicit: no more hacking, which is to say, no more earning a living at this "desk of a man who cannot be bought," etc.

Thank God I have a teaching assignment next semester. That may be a temporary solution. Meantime I fret and read and walk around Manhattan. Do you know about Ravel? In his last five years, he suffered from a brain tumor which gradually paralyzed his mind. One day his great friend Hélène Jourdan-Morhange visited him and found him sitting on his balcony at Montfort-L'Amaury. "What are you doing?" she asked, and Ravel looked down at her and replied, "*J'attends*."

Of course I'm not that badly off. I can still type. And I hope that if I assure my It that I won't ask him to do anything but write a story for 6 months, perhaps he'll unclench and play with me again.

Meantime we have had a glorious nor'easter, which came smashing through one of my front windows, hurtling broken glass and manic water all over me as I lay in bed. And I have dined with miss Lucia Marinetti—daughter of the futurist—elegant but too Milanese (business-minded) per me; and helped celebrate John Cage's 60th birthday, or birth-year; and listened to the election returns (but only until 10:30, after which I went back to my book-of-the-month, Quentin Bell's biography of his aunt Virginia Woolf. Superlative. Don't believe that dreary square on the front page of *The NY Times*.

Today our Jamaican maid Rosa is here, singing to herself, murmuring to the cat, and generally swabbing about. For lunch she only wants a pint of Häagen-Dazs ice cream—carob flavor, preferably. It's lovely here today—shiny-bright air, Viking blue sky, fire engines shrieking on Fifth Avenue, a letter from Aspen in the mailbox.

November 28
Aspen

Robertino,
Be mortified. Peggy Clifford, who for all we know will be famous—she's writing a series of six extraordinary programs for PBS TV on the failure of our dream life—Peggy Clifford is still asking me where is the copy of *The Literary Life* (if I have the title slightly wrong it's because she's had my cherished copy for the past five months). I told her you promised to have Farrar Straus send her one, believe me, to have her begging for a book is a considerable honor. Have them bill her for it, she's willing to pay, to do anything . . .

Your right hand is bad and my right eye. As someone said, it is bad because it is looking inward. I wish it were. I'm finishing this funny, I hope, film script. I'm supposed to bring it back to Italy about December 12. Now, this is a dumb question, but are you still going to Europe for Christmas, etc. and when and where are you going? Do you want to take the flight to Rome together on the 12th and stay at the as-far-as-I-know inexpensive and wonderful Inghilterra? I'll be in Rome for about 8–10 days, working, but we can all dine together, walk through the city in the warm part of afternoon, etc. etc. Please sign your acceptance in the space provided here:_________________ .

Speak to me, I am lonely. I have such tales of Venice and France!

. . .

Rackstraw Downes is a British artist, based in New York City. His style is regarded as realist. He is the recipient of a MacArthur Fellowship and is a member of the American Academy of Arts and Letters.

. . .

November 30
New York

Carissimo Giacomo,
Please apologize to Ms. Peggy Clifford for me. I have come back from the post office this minute and a copy of *The Lit Life* is en route . . . I remember your asking me to do this in 1971, or perhaps 1970. Mea culpa.

My God, if only I could go with you on the 12th! But it's impossible. Becki is going to Amsterdam (Vermeer country) on Christmas day for 3 weeks with Rackstraw Downes. Which means I'd have to be back the 24th *au plus tard*, since one of us has to be here to cat-sit. And no, no, I cannot visit Rome for the first time and spend barely a week—even if I could afford such caprices.

What I propose instead is this: from February to May 24 I have to teach. On May 26th—no May 28th, a Monday—I'm off to France. Now why couldn't we meet in Paris sometime in June, rent a car, and drive down the Loire Valley for 10 days? By then you'll have a whopping advance from Roger Straus for your novel and we can eat spring vegetables—and *fraises*!—and local cheese and read about Diane de Poitiers and Catherine de Medici and stag hunts etc. *Pense-y*.

Today, or tomorrow, with my shaky paw and scrawny wits, I must write, in French if possible though I don't think it will be, 3 pages for *Figaro Littéraire* on the *centenaire* of Madame Colette. Do Americans still read her, etc. Is it due to Audrey Hepburn? What can I say?

A man named Arthur Coppotelli has been in town this month. He translates (Marinetti) and worked with Pasolini on *Medea* and generally lives *la dolce vita* on the 6th floor of a palazzo near the Piazza Navona. He's looking for work and wants to be back "in time for the roses on my terrace, which is early March . . . "

December 15
Aspen

Caro Roberto,
I am listening to "Amazing Grace," the song that was played when they buried Karyl Roosevelt's daughter in the old Ute Cemetery. I suppose I've mentioned her, she is the ex-wife of Wm. Roosevelt, Franklin Delano's grandson, and her son, Nicky, who often stays with us (he's 12) is the great grandson. I find it an astonishing *saut* from the president whose name I first heard as a child playing on the New York streets and this young descendant playing touch football with me in the snows of Aspen. He's a very handsome boy, tough, good-hearted, and a fast runner . . .

I've felt, for a month, like those English of the Great War years, 1914_, who saw everyone they knew simply vanish and vanish forever. In the past few weeks a good friend from Chicago, Paul Rosenbluth, a doctor, died in his sleep suddenly (he was our age), Meta Burden who was so good-looking it was difficult to look at her was killed in an avalanche on the mountain that rises above us here, and Harvey Swados, to whom we were very close in Rockland County and later, in France, died on Monday of a stroke. I've been reading a little of Virginia Woolf by Clive Bell. How I love England, mainly I suppose because I've never known the heart of it.

The sun is pouring through the window onto my back, like a great hand encouraging me to go on. My daughter's Roman, marmalade cat (Kuna) has just leapt onto the table and is drinking my tea, these hours (it's in the morning) are the best of the day.

Thank you for sending the book. Yours in exile, yours in bliss,

J.

December 18
New York

Cher Jacques,
A hasty page, to tell you that Becki will be abroad until January 16th, therefore you are welcome to stay here en route and/or returning from Rome. Phone, bed, icebox, gin—no, misty Scotch—are all yours. Just let me know.

I was horrified by the news of Harvey's death. A brain hemorrhage. It was probably rage—at the injustice of the literary world vis-à-vis his twenty years' work. I heard a wretched story about his relations with Candida Di Dinadio and his last book—the big one, for which he thought he ought to have $100,000 in advance. He finally had to wait outside Miss D.'s elevator and demand his manuscript back. And he suffered so helplessly from this sense of ill-use that when Dan Wakefield told him his novel had been sold to Japan for $150, Harvey said he didn't want to hear about anyone else's foreign rights. He himself had never had any, not even European ones. A lifetime's indignation goeth before a hemorrhage. Harvey, pray for us.

Your letter was waiting when I stumbled out this morning to fight my way through Bloomingdale's children's department, trying to find Xmas presents for my niece and nephew. I wish they lived in Aspen instead of Scarsdale, as the ski paraphernalia were the only things that looked decent.

The Va. Woolf book is good—Bell's biography, I mean. The research is sound, but the point of view is personal and for once un-academic. Bell himself knew most of the dramatis personae and can speak with authority. Dorothea Straus [wife of publisher Roger Straus] assured me the marriage was never consummated—between Leonard and Virginia, that is; there seems to have been some sort of vaginal block, as with Queen Elizabeth I. But the relationship does not seem entirely non-carnal, as Bell's quotations from Virginia's letters present it. Glenway Wescott insists V. was an oragenital expert, since she once compared the odor of croci to male semen.

. . .

Sir Alan Bates was an actor, winner of an Academy Award for his work in The Fixer; *he also appeared in films such as* Women in Love *and* Zorba the Greek.

. . .

December 30
Aspen

Robertino,
Did you know there were two apartment houses near you where the waters of Minetta Brook, part of a beautiful island now vanished for 100 years, where these waters surface as fountains in the lobby? 33 Washington Square West and 2 Fifth Avenue.

Useless to make plans with these film people. I had already put my six notebooks in the safe-deposit box in the bank and was packing when, all excited, they called to say Alan Bates was supposed to be reading the script and if he did—this weekend—and liked it, why we would all meet in New York about the 14th. So back to the bank I went. What's wrong? they asked. I forgot something, I said, taking the books back home with me.

Have you read Gorky on Chekhov and Tolstoy? Marvelous details, long passages of conversation. "The coffin of the writer so 'dearly loved' by Moscow was brought in a green freight car labeled in huge letters on the side: FOR OYSTERS. A part of the crowd that had assembled at the station to meet the writer followed the coffin of General Keller, which had been brought from Manchuria at the same time, and was profoundly astonished to find that Chekhov was being buried with full military honors."

I have an injured ankle that I have to soak two or three times a day, I sit on the edge of the tub and read Gorky. Certain illnesses are a blessing.

Perhaps I'll see you about the 13th. I hope this actor catches a cold from the *Vogue* photographer and breaks out in fever blisters.

"Via Negativa" is in the new *Paris Review*, just arrived. I read it with yawns. It didn't stir the slightest feeling, somehow.

And as for you, I wish your right hand the calmness it needs and deserves, I would will it if I could.

1973 Imagine Finding a Friend Late in Life . . .

Salter went into 1973 with great confidence in the book that became Light Years. *He did not anticipate the difficulties he encountered with publishers, but these did not shake his belief in the book, not seriously. As for Phelps, he was told that he did in fact have Parkinson's disease. He seems stoic in the year's letters, though his reactions might be clearer if he had written more. The year was also notable for Phelps because he was able to travel to France, something he managed to do only a few times, despite his abiding love of the country and its writers. He also spent far less time writing book reviews and journalism, instead teaching at Manhattanville College. Perhaps it was all of these factors combined that caused Phelps to write only three letters to Salter in 1973; Salter wrote more frequently, and his letters show genuine concern for Phelps's health, as well as offering a maddening look at a work of fiction, so carefully crafted, being rejected out of hand.*

. . .

Charlotte Mew was an English poet. She published little during her lifetime, but Penelope Fitzgerald's book Charlotte Mew and Her Friends *generated renewed interest in her life and work.*

. . .

January 9
New York

Cher cadet,
I have a problem. As writer-in-residence at Manhattanville College next semester, I am giving a course called the Post-Novel. I had planned to begin point-blank with *A Sport and a Pastime*. But I have consulted

Bantam, who tell me it is no longer in print; nor do Brentano, Doubleday or even Bookazine have copies in stock. Would the author possibly have squirreled away two hundred copies, of which he would sell me, say, 10, at the original 95 cents apiece? I could even offer to return them, though they might be dog-eared and marginated by then. Or perhaps the Aspen bookstore still has a supply? Nepotism apart, the book would make a perfect launching pad for my semester's divagations, technical and otherwise. (When asked about my "philosophy" by the student paper last fall, I quoted Charlotte Mew: "the spirit afterward, but first the flesh . . . " So you see how appropriate *A Sport* would be the first couple of weeks) . . .

If you get here any time in January, we must try to get tickets for *Much Ado About Nothing*, with your quondam star Sam Waterston. The engagement has been extended through Feb. 4th.

I've finally consulted a neurologist about my aspen-paw and he told me that, after all, I have Parkinson's disease; psychosomatic imbalance (in my case, years of sexual clench, etc.) is the trouble.

Don't see *Deliverance*; a thalidomide baby; an ad-man's allegory out of Faulkner; not as bad as *El Topo* [a film by Alejandro Jorodowsky], but definitely in the running.

I'm reading Léautaud's letters and bits of Gadda. Did you know that Paul Scarron, a rheumatically lamed French poet of the 17th century, was the first husband (he died at 42) of Madamigella d'Aubigné, later known as Madame de Maintenon and, as Gadda endearingly puts it, the "second *moglie del Re Sole: la moglie morganatica*"?

. . .

In his January 12 letter, Salter refers to Richard Foreman's play The Magic Theater of Dr. Selavy. *It was actually entitled* Doctor Selavy's Magic Theater.

. . .

January 12
Aspen

Dear Rbto.,

How I wish I could write a letter like yours. I always feel like a child at camp: Yesterday we went hiking and I fell off a cliff . . .

Peggy Clifford came by to ask if it would be all right to thank you, by letter, for *The Literary Life*. I said, well, the maestro hates to be disturbed, especially when he is deeply engaged in his work, but perhaps a discreet letter, a letter in carpet slippers . . . she left, thanking me elaborately.

Last night, dinner with Ingo and Kate Preminger followed by what passes for excitement here: watching the first one-hour segment of a melancholy and inane work called *An American Family*. The creator must have been inspired by Jill Johnston—it was the most tedious, empty, false, banal thing imaginable. The crew filmed, I understand, some four or six hundred hours of this family (the Louds or Lowds). What we saw last night looked like the footage that was thrown away. Anyway Ingo was reminiscing about the early days with his wife—even before they were married. One of the first times she came to see him, he was at the gym. He had been boxing, his nose was bleeding.

"Of course, there was nothing unusual, he said. My nose is so large that if I am hit anywhere, it's on the nose."

They always serve excellent wine. As we sat down at the table, I said, "Dinner is a wonderful thing."

"I am getting used to it," he said agreeably.

I'm still waiting to hear about New York and Rome. I was to receive a call, without fail, yesterday, but of course there was none. Bates, it turns out, hasn't read the script, or as they euphemistically put it, "hasn't finished reading it." Someone described it to him and he isn't certain he wants to play a fat man.

Meanwhile I have a bad ankle, bursitis—someone kicked me—and I'm hobbling around like a man with the gout. Your suggestion that we go to the theater (!) stunned me. Of course I am willing to go, I'll see anything, even fat women dancing, the hungers that rise in one marooned here in the Alps are ferocious. I'd also like to see *The Magic*

Theater of Dr. Selavy. Unquestionably it will be a vast disappointment, but I'm doing it in the interests of your cultural improvement.

Unfortunately, much like the fables of all the world's peoples, I never expected the day when there would be no copies of *A Sport and a Pastime*, when it would be winter in the shops and even in Bookazine, I never put up copies for such a day. I have three Bantam copies that were sent to me originally, I'm sending them to you as well as two hardcover copies that were languishing on the shelf. The rest will have to come either from *The Paris Review*, which bought up all the extra Doubleday copies (or at least several hundred) or Fourth Avenue. Or I will copy out five more by hand, the prospect of readers, even readers who are fans of Kurt Vonnegut or think that the new journalism will sweep away all older and less vital forms of writing, such a prospect could drive me to extraordinary acts. You needn't return the copies, I have no use for them.

The Univ. of Massachusetts is establishing a Harvey Swados Scholarship Fund to provide support for a semester for students engaged in writing a story or a novel. I have the first 45 pages of my novel—I'm thinking, frivolously I suppose, of the title *Mohenjodaro*—ready and will bring them, perhaps I'll even bring 60 or 75 pages, to New York. I am imagining an advance and hoping to arouse interest. Have you seen *Les Maisons du Génie*, a book by Mme. Claude Arthaud? It will interest you.

Imagine finding a friend late in life when one's heart has begun to close. Your casual mention of Parkinson's disease disturbs me. Can you have a mild case of it? I'm reading *Dorland's Medical Dictionary*. Does the Laradopa quench the right hand's anguish? Is 3,000 mg a lot? What side effects? I must see you soon.

. . .

Charles Van Doren was the central figure in the 1950s NBC quiz show scandal. Mark Van Doren was an American poet. He earned the Pulitzer Prize in 1940 for his volume Collected Poems: 1922–1938.

. . .

April 28
Aspen

Dearest Robert,
Why haven't I written sooner? You've probably already gone, in the wake of Henry James, Goethe, Trelawney, Tennessee Williams and that witty man, Gore what's his name who's friends with so many people. I am awash with envy. Yes, I know I've been there, even this year, but one can't envy oneself.

I don't know when I wrote last, it was at least a month ago. Karyl Roosevelt's boyfriend, the young blond editor of the Chicago tabloid, was here for about ten days, oh, this was a while ago. He brought his children. They all stayed at her house. When she took the sheets from her bed to the Laundromat, the girl looked at her and said, "I don't know if I should wash these or call the police."

Karyl was also subject to a half-hearted approach by Chas. van Doren, perhaps you know him, he was here about Easter time. He still seemed to know the answers to all the questions. We were talking at dinner about the revolt of each generation in America, a revolt which he said could be found nowhere else in the world. I said that it was because of a deep longing to change our lives. You want to change your life? he asked. Oh, yes, Karyl cried—she was sitting next to him—I would give anything, anything in the world to change mine. Well, van Doren said, I wouldn't—he was very emphatic, the assertion of someone who must defend something at all costs—I wouldn't change a single thing, he said, not one thing. Later I heard him confiding to her—we were on to other things—all men are liars and cheats.

But he did know John Berryman and even told me the name of the English girl Berryman had loved so much, all his life I believe, it was a marvelous name but I've forgotten it. Berryman seems a little like [the poet John] Betjeman to me, that is, he is a pond. I can imagine them classmates at some good school, one wild, the other loving and envious. I'm reading *Love and Fame* [a book by Berryman], which is very warm and even funny. Mark van Doren is often mentioned, he apparently felt towards Berryman as towards a son.

When are you leaving? Is it by boat? Will you write to me? I'll be here, trying to finish my book by July. I have a garden to build before then and also a shack to repair in which my daughter who has decided to forget school for the present and perhaps longer would like to live in next fall and winter. I also expect to see the first crop of Corgis. My scrawny little bitch, she should be named Lolita, is coming into her second heat.

Love to Becki. And to you, memorable days.

. . .

Howard Moss was an American poet. His Selected Poems *(1971) earned both the Pulitzer Prize for Poetry in 1971 and the National Book Award for Poetry in 1972. Louise de Vilmorin was a French novelist, poet, and journalist. Her best-known work was the novel* Madame de. *Mary Cantwell was a writer and journalist, the author of three volumes of memoir now collected as* Manhattan Memoir.

. . .

May 15
New York

Cher Cadet,
C'est décidé. J'arrive à Paris le matin du 23 pour un mois de flâner, marcher, pleurer, manger, aller a la dérive.

I'm tired, it seems. I've enjoyed my three months as guru at Manhattanville, but I've worked hard. Two weekly lectures, three writing workshops, drunken faculty, three "special" students (without talent); and having to tote a suitcase full of books and clean socks and T-shirts etc. out to Purchase every Sunday afternoon and back Tuesday evening.

I want a change and a rest.

What can I do for you in the 6th arrondisement? I have no plans. I'll probably stay at the Quai Voltaire—(1) because I have no originality, and (2) because I love the view of the Pavillion de Flore. There will be an exhibit of manuscripts of Colette at the Bibliothèque Nationale. A friend of mine—Jean Chalon—has just published a book about Louise de Vilmorin (see this month's *Elle*) and he'll show me around a bit. I expect to see the new version of Gluck's *Orpheus and Eurydice* at Rolf Liebermann's opera. And several people whom I never see in New York—e.g. Howard Moss and Ned Rorem—will be there and we'll have lunch. Otherwise I'll prowl and read my *Guide Littéraire de la France* and try to hold my right hand steady enough to send you a big "X" on a postcard.

I come back June 20th. Then almost at once to Maine for a month. Then, all of August, back to my job at Manhattanville: ten lectures (three hours each) on "The Quality of Life in Modern Literature." Or maybe it's the Life of Quality etc. Or the Modernity of Life. Fraud, but I'll work hard; please the Westchester ladies; and pay my baffled way.

This evening—it's now 7 P.M.—my martini is almost gone—and a dinner guest is due—I have to write 750 words on "any book you love" for *Mlle.*: @ $150. Pays for the raincoat and drip-dry shirts and black underwear I bought at Bloomingdale's yesterday.

Bless your work-in-progress. There are three girls at Manhattanville who adore you, at least the author of *A Sport and a Pastime*.

I have never met Charles Van Doren and I was not a television viewer in the days of his grandeur. But I once saw him walking down Hudson Street and he looked haunted. I've not yet read *Love and Fame*, but I esteem Berryman very highly.

Lunching at Le Cheval Blanc on some 25 tasty mussels yesterday, I found myself staring up at a middle-aged man who smiled, presented his card, and said he was Ivan Obolensky. My first publisher! *Mais où sont les éditeurs d'antan*? And the lady with me, Mary Cantwell of *Mlle.*, said, "Oh but his uncle was very rich, wasn't he?"

Did you know that St. Francis of Assisi thought of God "as a melody, so sweet that it could just be borne"? One of his best friars, Giles, when attacked by theologians, answered their arguments on the flute. (*A Calendar of Saints for Unbelievers*, by Glenway Wescott, a dear book which that earnest scold, Miss Mary McCarthy, once called "smug, trivial aphoristic skepticism.")

. . .

Elsa Martinelli, an Italian actress and one-time fashion model, has appeared in films such as the Orson Welles-directed The Trial *(1962) and* Candy *(1968) alongside Marlon Brando and John Huston, among others.*

. . .

May 16
Aspen

So, dear Robert, you are off. I can see that everything has been carefully arranged, you are a man who takes care of things. After all, didn't I watch you packing for your trip to Purchase, everything thought of, everything in its place. I wish I were going but I'm happier that you are. You will be nourished by France, I would only wander around like a figure in a Jean Rhys book. Well, even so, I've written to Maxine Groffsky that you are coming, she's *The Paris Review* lady, etc. etc. I'm sure you know all about her, she's bought a marvelous little flat near the Odeon on a street that is like a 1920 Lartigue photo. There's a brasserie not far off that is her brasserie, it's not Lipp but it's just as good-looking, the table cloths are white, there is the pleasing murmur of conversation and the ring of forks. The name of this oasis is the Brasserie Balzar, 49 rue des Ecoles . . .

Also I'm telling Huguette Faget that you'll be in Paris. She's a wonderful woman, lives on Place St. Sulpice and helps run a People's Theatre and Cinema Center in Vincennes whence she goes daily on her bicycle (45 minutes). She knows writers, directors, publishers, she was an actress . . .

An ex-NY girl who married a Frenchman, divorced, has lived in Paris for 15 years, does some journalism, very nice, very funny, very intelligent is Barbara Aptekman. She's a very good friend—she was Stanley Donen's girl when I stayed *chez* Donen that summer. Her flat is, as they used to say, to die.

Elsa Martinelli, say you are bringing my love . . .

If you have a chance, eat one evening at Chez Benoit, 20 rue St. Martin (very near the river, maybe it's Blvd. St. Martin, no I just looked it up: rue). Classic bistro, prices have gone up a little but a wonderful place.

Balzac died in 24 Avenue Fortune, Proust at 44 rue Hamelin, Victor Hugo's houses in Paris included:

2 rue des Vielles Thuilleries
18 rue des Petits Augustins
10 rue des Mezieres
30 rue du Dragon
12 rue du Cherche-Midi
90 rue de Vauginard
11 rue Notre Dame des Champs
9 rue Jean-Goujon
6 Place Royale
5 rue de l'Italy
37 rue de la Tour d'Auvergne
5 Ave. Frochet
66 rue de la Rochefoucauld
55 rue Pigalle
21 rue de Clichy
130 Avenue d'Eylan

And of course, his house and museum in the corner of the Place des Vosges—don't miss it. His first child was born in 1824, his last in 1868 (!). I'm sending off 185 pages of my book today all nicely typed. How I would like to be able to read it for the first time. *Bon voyage mon vieux.* You will have a marvelous time.

. . .

The writer Brendan Gill was a longtime contributor to The New Yorker. *John Simon was the theater critic for* New York Magazine *from 1968 until 2005. He continues to write criticism. Herman Wouk is an American writer, the winner of the Pulitzer Prize and author of* The Caine Mutiny, The Winds of War, *and* War and Remembrance, *among other works.*

. . .

July 1
Still Aspen

Cher Robert,
You have either vanished into the provinces like certain archetypes of fiction or the dollar has dropped so far you can't pay your way home. My own experience has been that I write letters from abroad when lonely or idle and I judge you have been little of either. I did have a letter from Maxine Groffsky saying yes, yes, by all means have this *mensch* call me, I am working out of my roofgarden usually, my number is such and such or call *The Paris Review* office—I'm certain you didn't, you snail.

Here it is thunderously hot, even the flies are stunned and the trees as if drugged. I am content. I am alone in the house except for three cats and my dog, not to count other insignificant—in terms of size—creatures. My wife and three daughters are in Sag Harbor until the end of the month. My son is in a camp on the Colorado River. I don't know if I am working any better but I am certainly feeling better. Solitude is grace providing you are living in the right spot. I have been reading [André] Maurois' *Proust* and working from about eleven to three or three-thirty. Not one publisher (Athenaeum, Random House, Holt-Rinehart, Viking) would give me a decent advance on the 185 pages I finally showed them. One turned me down definitely. There was some encouragement. Joe Fox at Random said please don't show it around any more—wait until it's finished and I can probably get you the advance you want. He didn't say it to me. Not one of them sent me a note of even one line. I'm not really bitter, nor even greatly disappointed. It would be very nice, though, to have the book succeed. I do like it enormously. I'm about 60% finished. A fruitful month here would be wonderful. Some of the best parts are still ahead. At least I always believe that.

Tell me about France, a letter of many pages. Brendan Gill and John Simon (are they friends of yours?) were both here. Gill brought pornographic films which he described in a lovely, eloquent, and somewhat old-fashioned speech ("My first given . . . ") as being failed art, but still worthy, still on the affirmative side of life, and perhaps the precursors of a real art. He then showed *The Devil in Miss Jones*, a piece of absolute trash but quite explicit. Beside me was sitting a white-haired man in a small-brimmed hat with a sweater tied across his shoulders like a camper, and his wife in a Bendel coat. Before the speech, while we were waiting, he turned to me—the crowd was enormous—and said: This is my first day in Aspen. What is this? The design conference, I said. How nice. It was Herman Wouk. He left without comment.

July 12
Cape Porpoise, Maine

Dear, dear James,
Where can I begin? It's July. I'm looking out on a blue estuary. I can hear gulls and wild ducks. I eat clams and lobster. I'm reading Miss Sarah Orne Jewett (whose *Country of the Pointed Firs* seems to me to be the great American novel, after all) and thanks to the bright sea light, my cat's eyes are almost entirely yellow iris, the pupils being reduced to the merest slits of eager black. Becki makes seascapes and landscapes and estuary-scapes by the dozen. She is also suffering from a monstrous rash—"hives-like"—which appeared out of nowhere two days ago and which we treat with cortisone spray, if you please.

Nevertheless I bring you the love of Huguette Faget, a noble soul whom I saw too little of, alas, but whose valiant Théâtre du Tempête I did at least (unlike you) visit. Paris was more beautiful than I'd remembered. The self-respect, the physical beauty, the allure, of the natives are stunning. A slouching, uncertain American can be recognized two blocks away—by the droop of the shoulder, the sag of the waistline, the shamble of the leg. The French, young and old, males and females, are the most elegant, self-assured, straight-backed and handsome people on the planet today. And prosperous, and clean and shapely—with shining hair and insolent eyes; a race of toreadors—I've never seen so many twinkling ankles, flat stomachs, unbrassiered bosoms, knowing behinds. What a place to watch the human creature at his apogee! And what a polymorphous voyeur I turned out to be! A glass of kir, a sidewalk seat and thou, *jeunesse de France*! *C'est le comble*.

I also worked. Taxi-ed out to Malmaison and interviewed Maître Jouhandeau for hours and days. He lives in his tiny Swiss chalet on the grounds of Napoleon's first wife's chateau; with a Spanish chauffer and a French cook and his 11-year-old *fils adoptif* named Marc who plays with toy sports cars on the floor while Marcel sits at his table and chronicles what he sees, remembers, feels, and is told by visitors (Jünger—the German Hemingway—one day; an old lover the next; me in between).

I sprained an ankle (dashing down a flight of cellar stairs to get another bottle of Fleuris). This was in Beaumont-du-Gâtinais, where Colette's daughter has a house and three or four walled-in acres of potage, rose gardens, lawn, pigeons, cat, dog (named Saucisson); and practices an art de vivre at which a poor Puritanical American such as I can only marvel. And how I ate! For instance at a certain inn (the courtyard tumbling with roses) called l'Ecu in Malesherbes! Or at your own Balzar where I had a memorable *lapin chasseur* one Sunday, surrounded by fascinatingly proper, elderly bourgeoisie who knew how to eat. I moved several times—staying one night in Colette's *chambre rouge* at the Palais Royal, another in the rue Vaneau, opposite Gide's house—but mostly remained at the Quai Voltaire, which is *bruyant*, but has the most exhilarating view I know in Paris: the Pont Royal and the pont du Carrousel, the Louvre, the Coupole, the dome of the Grand Palais to the west, and 180 degrees of Paris sky, as well as the glittering Seine below. I neglected tourist duties, but met lots of people and literally lost 8 lbs trying to speak and understand French. I read it so much of the time here in America that I have the illusion that I can speak it as well. I can't, of course, and discovering this was an awful blow to my self-esteem. But I managed somehow, though six successive hours of listening to Maître Jouhandeau was more exhausting than any physical labor I've ever undertaken. (With him, by the way, I had one of my most extraordinary meals: a *tête de veau* and the *cervelles* after, along with a bottle of '61 Burgundy—and at a bistro in Courbevoie—*c'est à dire*, the nether Bronx—a bistro owned and operated by a man, now in his forties, who was circa 1950 Jouhandeau's great love and about whom he has written a masterpiece called *Du Pur Amour*: The lunch was cooked by the beloved hero's wife—a great beauty—and served by his own hands. (He also very proudly autographed a copy of the book!)

Thank you for your letters, addresses, affection, advice. How is the book? Huguette and I talked about you a great deal, and she loves *Three* and *A Sport* almost as much as I do. She told me she still has Peugeot #2 in the south of France somewhere. She seems fulfilled and certainly has a busy life which she believes in. When will you be in NY again? I'll be back at 12th St. August 1st. I have to give 10 lectures in August! Ugh. I'll write again shortly. It's 11:30. Tide is in (there is nothing more dramatic than the daily tides) and I'm famished, having been up since 5:30. Thank you again. I thought of you every day I was in Paris.

. . .

Frances FitzGerald is an American journalist. Her book Fire in the Lake: The Vietnamese and Americans in Vietnam *(1972), was awarded both the Pultizer Prize and the National Book Award.*

. . .

July 19
Aspen

Darling boy. Your delicious letter reached me just before the weekend. I read it entire, I then read parts of it to various people and, forgetting to have it with me, recited from memory certain parts. To S. Bellow I told about the meal in Courbevoie, *tête de veau*, served by the owner's own hands. "You can lead a *tête de veau*," he murmured, "but you can't make him drink," . . . So much for the mighty. He's been reading to me from his new book (in progress) which is redolent of *Herzog*, at least it has that assurance, wit and richness, and has invited me to show him my work, but I haven't. Instead I plod onward, sometimes going to bed with a warm feeling, sometimes sick from failure. I've about 350 pages, which is ⅔ of it. I have to finish it or starve. There is absolutely nothing else to see us through the coming year, although I suppose I could go back on the streets, although again, when you need money they know it and won't give you work. That's, as they say, the way the game is played. From Roger Straus I have come to expect nothing. From Random House I am hoping for a $15,000 advance which once seemed a lot but now, after fees, taxes, etc. will only stretch six or seven months. Bellow again. We were talking about advances, editors, etc. and I mentioned—I had heard this in New York—that Philip Roth had received $500,000 for the hardback rights only to his baseball manual. "What hath Roth gott," he sighed. We were with Frances FitzGerald that night, it was in The House of Lum, it could have been Elaine's.

I've just given away three copies, freshly bought, of course, of *Earthly Paradise*.

I loved your trip to France.

Becki, I embrace thee. The night deepens.

August 6
Aspen

Dear Roberto,
Beautiful days here, the land has never been so green. Bellow is leaving in a week, he was going to stay the month but he has to go back to face his bitch ex-wife in a lawsuit, she wants $25,000 a year in perpetuity, whether she remarries or not, he has vowed to go to prison first. Further she's the head of Women's Lib(!) in her area. Anyway he's coming for lunch today. He likes salmon.

The great disappointment is that my dog is not pregnant. I had already announced her puppies and taken for myself the largest of the males, I named him Sumo. Now there is to be nothing. We are seriously depressed.

I am supposed to receive in the next day or so pages 235–380 which are now being typed. I have twelve more chapters to write of some fifty-four. It's still my dream to finish by Labor Day. A *New Yorker* writer named Ed Epstein who's published two books at Viking and one at Random House asked me who my publisher would be. I didn't know. The best in New York, I said. The best in New York, he said, is unquestionably Farrar Straus. Well, of course, that plunged me into gloom given Roger Straus's off-handed comments about the first chapters I showed him, but then I'm relying upon you to mention to him that in my mind he is the shah of shahs, and to reawaken in him an interest in me and mine.

If the truth be known, I am thirsting fame. I am also doing a good bit of gardening. The lettuces are so thick we can't eat them fast enough, two beautiful shades of green. The pebble walks I laid are wet with rain.

September 15
Aspen

Robert, my son. An autumn morning, I am drinking Twining's Orange Tea preparatory to beginning work on the old tool and coal shed I'm renovating for the winter occupancy of my oldest daughter who would like some privacy this year and who is helping me in a sort of sunbathing way. The shed will be lovely and snug though the amount of work that goes into these good looks and snugness is enormous, especially when undertaken alone. My young son, the child I really adore—we have, I don't think I'm deceiving myself, a great mutual love, mine will last longer, I suppose—is helping me on the weekends and will be there today. Old boards, curling shavings from the plane, measurements, all in the autumn sunshine, it isn't bad.

Yvonne, I think, has gone. We had one, brief picnic with her on her plantation here, she seemed less falsely modest and concealed this year, a kind of urgent frankness was seeking to break out as if she realized time was growing shorter. She wants to sell her apartment near the Met and move to Soho. Vivi is living in Cleveland (!) and singing in Cincinnati, I think. Her husband is teaching.

I've just had a letter from Doubleday. They're taking another story of mine for the forthcoming O. Henry Collection (1974), this will be the third, I've yet to win a prize, even a third prize, I suppose it will be J. C. Oates again. I think you read this story, it's "Via Negativa," written two years ago, that's how long it takes Plimpton to publish, etc. etc. The wonderful thing about the O. Henry Collection, for a year or two after there arrive semi-annual checks for twelve dollars or so.

I've been reading a battered, library copy of *Sido and My Mother's House* (what a story about the books her father, Capt. Colette, never wrote, the bound, titled volumes with their touching dedications and blank pages they found after his death). It's Secker and Warburg. Is there an in-print U.S. edition of these two, together or separately? I'd love to have it. Did you know that Edward Hamilton, bookseller, is remaindering *The Literary Life* at $4.95 in his huge new catalog? I'm buying several, of course. I've given them to everyone I know but there's always the possibility of meeting someone new.

Écoute, I have 475 pages of my book, I'm on the last three chapters, with one final summoning of will, I can finish this coming week. I don't know if you'll want to read it, I myself hate to devote myself to anything about which there is any question, not because I'm mean or narrow but because I read so little and am demoralized by bad books, but I would like Robert Giroux to read it. I was advised here by a man who seemed to know what he was talking about, come to think of it, it was Saul Bellow, that Giroux had excellent taste and was the real literary intelligence at FSG. Now, you know, that it is Rog. Straus with whom I have been indolently flirting there the last three or four years and who, having read the perhaps too brief, first 50 pages, wrote that he could see nothing here to become excited about. I'd like to approach Giroux without ruining my chances by affronting Roger. How can I do this? Surely there must be some way. I must tell you there are times when I absolutely adore this book and I think a worthy publisher might not be disappointed.

Meanwhile, St. Clement's Theater, ex-American Place, is definitely putting on a prepared reading of my play on November 11, 12, and 13th. Does your invitation to stay *chez toi*, often discussed, never become reality, still hold? If I stayed, would I ruin your daily schedule and life?

They say they're going to rehearse for two weeks before putting it on, and these two weeks I ought to be there. In these lean times, I have been staying at my mother's, but I absolutely can't do that while working on the play, I can hardly keep my personality intact at my mother's much less concentrate on anything else. Perhaps this visit would, in the fullness of time, as they say, become historic. Becki keeps saying that each year is going to be the year for me, she's eventually got to be right.

The West German chancellor, Willi Brandt, and his good friend, G. Grass, are coming here two weeks from today. Brandt to receive a humanitarian award and $10,000 and probably to deliver an address. I have an invitation to the proceedings and am eager to see them (the personages) in life.

Now, off to the lumberyard. With dog.

December 3
Snow on the ground, silence at last

Dear friend, companion, man,
The train is marvelous beyond compare. The sense of melancholy and security as you set out across the flatlands of New Jersey, through its filthy industrial backyards, evening falling. All the cars have been completely refurbished, it's a royal train, breathlessly clean, the sleeves of the waiters fresh, the food inexpensive, the service good. In the morning at seven o'clock, reflected in the curve of the upper berth metal above my head was a rush of green like the sea—the misty fields of Illinois, the dark trees, the farmland endlessly passing. And the station in Chicago is right in the heart of the city. Well, all the wonders of travel were known to an earlier age, but it's good to know they haven't completely disappeared.

I spent the morning in the Chicago Art Institute which has a really fine—the best in the country, I'm told—collection of impressionists, including a portrait of the three-year-old Jean Renoir painted by his Da, what is so thrilling about it is he still looks exactly like it. There's a ravishing Degas, *In the Millinery Shop* (sic), and a huge Matisse, *Bathers by the River*, better than any of the others I've ever seen. I had in one hand a copy of [Hugh] Morrison's *Louis Sullivan* bought at the Met in New York, and went to see his famous Auditorium Building which is really an ugly heap and the Carson, Pirie, Scott store, more beautiful but still not art. I would have liked to visit the Graceland Cemetery and seen the monuments there, but I had to meet Saul Bellow in the aquarium. We strolled among the eels and drowsing fishes and then drove to his cousin's bakery, all the while he gave me his reactions and thoughts about my book. I found them exact, well-taken, I have been sleeping on them, along with others, sleepless on them would be more truthful, for weeks.

It would be better if shorter, he said. Its repetitiousness causes it to lose power. I am perhaps a little too indulgent toward the people, and the book would be better if the angles were sharper. When something exceptional happens in a novel, one wants to know whether the writer understands it or not, he said. And perhaps most interesting, at the end, he said the book was really about the sexual heartlessness of women—their new role—the *vita nova* for women and they are devastating in it. Of course, this surprised me, coming last, because it brought everything down to earth again, made it real, human. He sees in the book one of his principal obsessions or at the least, hoarded ideas, and while I recognize, even acknowledge this to some extent, still it means he is evaluating the book in a special way or partially in a special way. He's the only reader, too, to call the Italian woman Viri marries "lovely and enchanting." Almost everyone else dislikes her, sometimes fiercely.

Joe Fox is coming out on the 22nd and will stay for 10 days. I expect to discuss everything then and afterwards go to work as if reading it for the first time myself. I no longer have any emotional attachment to it, I merely want it to have good proportions, so to speak, when it goes forth.

James Michie of Bodley Head is reading it. It was given to him by Fox. If he likes it, that will of course be very encouraging to Fox, not to speak of me.

Of everything in New York, I loved the lunch with you at the Russian Tea Room best. I tried to write some of it down, my notes are all scribbled and disorganized. A book which had been floating around vaguely in my mind—I know its title and its end—alighted during that lunch, came to rest, within reach or almost within reach and I woke up at three in the morning afterwards and began writing feverishly. When I reached home I took out a thin, handsome sketchbook, an English notebook of Winsor and Newton that I had been keeping until I had the courage to write on its pages, and began copying things down. It's by my elbow now. Somewhere in that book when I finish it will be our lunch, redecorated, reassigned, but very recognizable, I think.

I love your stories.

Cynthia Buchanan wrote quite a nice one, a description really, in a recent *Newsweek*. Was she your student? I forget.

Last night at dinner there was a grandson of Louise de Vilmorin, he's seventeen, very nice, and here for the winter working in a small hotel, the proprietor of which I know and who I think will not pay him, but no matter. He's out of Loomis and accepted at Harvard, but has decided to postpone his entrance there for a year. His name is Edmund Hersey. He demonstrated how his grandmother sat (always with one knee on the floor and a hand at her throat) and imitated the voice of Malraux. Intimacy is always fascinating, especially intimacy with gods. He's coming next week to cook dinner for us, he says he's quite good.

I have my desk cleared and my notebooks, etc., from *The Death Star* ready to put on it and open.

You are my beacon, my idea of life. When I saw the size of the tip you left for the waitress at the Tea Room, I realized how much I still have to learn.

1974 Samizdat Lives

Phelps wrote only one letter to Salter in 1974. In that letter, he apologizes and discounts the excuses he could use, instead saying he feels "posthumous" and wonders if falling in love with one of his students might "bring my posthumousness to an end." It is unclear whether this silence was owed to his grappling with the Parkinson's diagnosis from the previous year, or was simply due to the combination of teaching duties and deadlines. Salter faced continuing doubts—publishers' doubts, not his own—about his new novel. He also wrote a play, Poisonous Soil, *which was never produced, and did some writing for films, though his feelings toward Hollywood are particularly clear in one letter from the year.*

January 1
Aspen

Dearest Robert, dearest Rosemarie,

Bonne anneé. There's no use wishing that one year will be better than others, but we cling to these ideas. Joe Fox has been here for a week, he's leaving today (if the Blizzard doesn't strike again—we've had four days of terrible, enormous snow). As usual, the substantial part of all our talking took place during the last 30 minutes in the bar of the Jerome, the plate glass windows steaming on the inside. He gave the book to two other readers at Random House, both women (as I suggested), one an editor, the other a copy editor he admires a lot, both of them liked it tremendously. As you know, it's been my suspicion that its dimensions and tone are more appealing to women. So far there's only one woman of six who didn't like it.

Random will publish it next January–February. I'll begin revisions in March when he and the copy editor return the manuscript to me with their complete commentary. They're giving a $7,500 advance—I think I've told you that. Like a paroled convict, I am grateful, and I harbor resentment.

I have burning a huge fire; it's cold anyway. I am reading the most odious, self-serving book ever: Hotchner's *Papa Hemingway*, I don't know why, to fan myself into a fury, I suppose.

Eva Marie Saint is coming to dinner tonight, she really is a very funny, charming woman; how she's aged!

I am expecting a great work out of you, composed as you suggest largely of irresistible footnotes, a book of digressions accurate as darts. I am preparing to share you with the world.

Sickness is health.

. . .

*Salter's anecdote about the actor Gregory Ratoff (*All About Eve*) is a highlight of this letter. His closing mention of a story about the making of* The Hustler, *which is "too long and detailed for now," reminds the reader that for all the compelling things Salter and Phelps committed to the page, their conversations were richer still—and that we were, unfortunately, not party to them.*

. . .

January 11
Aspen

Illustrious friend, brother, poet/Poet:
Salut!

Where are you?

Yesterday, furious as a carpenter hammering in nails that keep bending, I finished rewriting the play. It's a new woman, as they say.

It's being typed by a slow-witted child in some lawyer's offices here. She has a fabulous machine, an IBM almost three feet long, it hardly makes a sound; it cruises like a limousine . . .

My neighbor Ingo Preminger came to dinner last night, he told stories about Gregory Ratoff who called him "Inga." Ratoff was summoned back from Europe to appear in a "Joe Mankywitz" film (*All About Eve*). He waited three weeks in Hollywood, finally he received a call, "Come to San Francisca" where the film is being made. Years later, at the theatre, Ratoff was sitting behind him and in the middle of a performance he heard a heartbreaking, "Inga! Help me!" Ratoff was having a heart attack. Ingo managed to carry him (he was enormously stout) to a dingy little manager's office where he laid him on the floor, grey as newsprint, dying, but he didn't die. Also about the making of *The Hustler*, wonderful story, too long and detailed for now.

I long to hear from you, there is no substitute.

February 13
Malibu, redolent of '30s life
With Gatsby

Caro Roberto,
How empty the Pacific mornings are. D'Annunzio would have loved Southern California. Sun, elegant young women driving silver cars. I often repeat a line I heard from you: the youth of my old age. Redford's house is on the beach here. Like all great rulers, he sleeps badly. He lives in a haughty, casual style. Yesterday he was reading his journals from *Gatsby* to me. I was depressed—he's not a bad writer, he observes with great shrewdness, even wit. A line about his wife—they had bumped into a production chief who has having an affair with a script girl. He was embarrassed, he thought Lola Redford would think less of him, even scorn him, "She somehow manages to give this impression," Redford writes.

The fever has passed for me. It's almost as if I'd lived this life and even achieved something in it. Last night we had dinner with two producers, husband and wife. I had once met her in the corridors of Paramount in New York where she was an assistant story editor. Now, she's produced *The Sting*. It takes a lifetime to completely fall but only a single stroke to rise. How completely, how naturally she has become a person of importance, a monarch, her wings have dried and straightened in one season, she has the confidence, the candor of one born. Even her hair is now fine and gleaming.

In my hand, to protect me, I have Nadezhda Mandelstam's *Hope Against Hope*. The only Mandelstam they know out here is a member of a law firm. I'm here to testify in a lawsuit, an old nuisance suit from *Downhill Racer*. Redford is everywhere admired, recognized, asked for his autograph. Even our lawyer begs me for anecdotes about him. The ocean is blue, unending. An old woman saw it for the first time, arriving in a bus—the driver stopped on a hill. "There it is," he said. "Is that it?" she said, "Funny, I thought it would be bigger."

I've signed my Random House contract. I'm determined to make that book something only a few people believe it can be. I miss you. I send you my real thoughts and love.

. . .

A Poet's Alphabet *was a book by Louise Bogan.*

. . .

March 23
Aspen

Caro Roberto,
Of everyone not writing to me, you are the most.

I love *A Poet's Alphabet*. I'm reading Peggy Clifford's copy. I'm also reading Evelyn Waugh, delicious writer and, to my mind, inept, at least he is in *The Sword of Honor* trilogy which has all the ingredients but Waugh just doesn't know how to make them unforgettable, and after all, that's the whole idea, isn't it? He is too off-handed. He is too diffuse. Still, I'm glad to have discovered him. Discovered Waugh? You are thinking, good God, next he'll be discovering Thomas Hardy.

My manuscript is due back from Random House for revisions in June. I've been thinking, probably idly, of going off with it to work for a month. Could I endure a place such as Porpoise Bay in June? Do you know comfortable lodgings there? It's either there, Long Island, or Key West, and I don't have a house offered to me in any of the three. Or Cape Cod, I suppose. There, either. Probably my family won't let me go. The older they get, the more difficult and consuming they are . . .

Gogol was born on the 1st of April, 1809. Beckett the next day, ninety-seven years later. I could live such a good life next time. It's so unfortunate there won't be any. I think of your mother falling to her knees and weeping in the path leading back to the house.

Speak.

April 27
New York

Dear James,

By my count, it's six letters I owe you. Along with assorted apologies, explanations, excuses, all scrupulously formulated as I dashed up the stairs with an armload of seltzer water and navel oranges, or stumbled down the stairs grappling with sacks of laundry, or hurtled along Union Square west with this or that chore for our publisher (a blurb for Mlle. [Marguerite] Yourcenar's book, a hasty translation from the French of Solzhenitsyn's text for a picture book, etc.), or staggered through Grand Central on my way to Purchase and my weekly lectures (Pavese last Tuesday, Tolkien coming up).

But this is a half-truth. I have had time—there's always time. I've simply been semi-comatose; menopausal; climacteric; dormant; between-the-acts, so to speak. I can barely remember the past two years. It's as though I haven't yet lived them. Some days I feel posthumous, as though I had died in the fall of 1971, while I was visiting Willa Cather's grave near the MacDowell Colony.

So you must forgive my "missing dates" ("The waste remains, the waste remains and kills . . . "). I think of you lovingly, gratefully, enviously, peevishly, benignly every day, especially at martini time.

As for local news: as usual, I am overdue—this morning, in particular, with a memoir-ette of Jim Agee, promised to a publisher 6 months ago. My problem here is that I have so little material. The editor wants "anecdotes." Ach. On the other hand, I seem to have discovered a new author (for me, that is): Ivy Compton-Burnett, whose father was a homeopath, who described herself as sexually a "neuter," and who died in 1969 at 85 leaving 19 books and 15,000 pounds to keep them in print. I have tried unsuccessfully to read her since about 1951. This week, to my surprise and moderate joy, I am in the middle of *A Family and a Fortune*.

I've had a good lunch with Thom Gunn, the British poet who lives in San Francisco (where he used his recent Guggenheim as the deposit on a house), dresses in faded Levi's and leather, and knows all about poets like Fulke Greville who was killed by his valet while at stool. I had an even better lunch (including some April shad roe) with a lady named Lola Szladits who directs the Berg collection of rare books and mss. at the NY Public Library. I saw Va. Woolf's diaries, Tillie Olsen's handwriting (which has to be read with a large magnifying glass), a lovely letter from Aldous Huxley to D. H. Lawrence describing a lesbian nightclub with two giant lady wrestlers, etc.

Small pleasures, temperate delights. It's spring today, fresh, blue, shining, tulip trees in bloom. I keep looking at my students (40 at the New School, another 40 at Manhattanville) and urging myself to fall in love with one or two. It might bring my posthumousness to an end.

Meantime I have 2 new dictionaries. Bless you.

Robert

P.S.: Of the titles [for the book that became *Light Years*], I think I like *Vita Nova* best; then *Estuarial Lives*. What does *Samizdat* mean?

P.S.S.: Peter Deane is taking over the little wellshaft room downstairs as a Manhattan office. He has lent me his binoculars, with which I have become an apprentice voyeur to East 12th Street, looking west to Fifth Avenue, not to mention several floors of glassy *Women's Wear Daily* offices immediately opposite.

May 1
Aspen

What a grand relief to hear from you. No need to count the letters, yours are worth two or three of mine. There's so little to write about from here. I've read I. Compton-Burnett; it was so long ago I can't even remember what it was like. I opened one of her books at Peggy Clifford's last night to have a little reminder and I promptly toppled into deathlike sleep. What I am reading is Virginia Woolf's *Between the Acts*. Quite dazzling.

I'm reading it as a kind of convalescence. I just finished a play. It has some lovely things in it, but I don't know whether it's any good or not; I need to fall back ten or twenty miles and have a look at it. I'm hoping it will provide you with some perfect sleep one evening next winter, possibly at a little better house than St. Clements. It's called *Poisonous Soil*.

Samizdat—I am shocked, don't you ever read *The NY Review*?—are the manuscripts passed around hand to hand in Russia, I think of them as being onionskin, as contrasted to the legitimately published. They are underground literature, unheralded literature, secret but most valuable. You and I are leading Samizdat lives . . .

I am in a state of staggering confusion about the title. I seize on one, embrace it ecstatically, then look again and say, what am I thinking of? Don't you have an old one, very nice but which you have no use for, hanging around? Be well. Multiply.

May 30
Aspen

Dear Robert,

In early morning on a rock out in the meadow which is still cool when the sun is warm I've been reading, for the first time from start to finish, your marvelous book. It makes me bow my head. My dog sleeps in the shade, a piece of raspberry-colored yarn around his big neck and tied in a bow—my children's birthday party was last night. Colette is such a beautiful writer. I stood in the Palais Royal a year and a half ago and thought about her: I've read half of *Earthly Paradise* now, in order. What a voyage! What evenings! What dawns! There is a way for words to go together which is invincible. And a way in which to live which will not stale.

As for myself, I am miserable. I have three or four good hours a day, the rest is rage or just complete indifference. And what happens during those three or four hours? I suppose I write. Sometimes I sit in the sun with the five new puppies and let them chew my shoelaces. What faces they have, what purity in their eyes!

Karyl Roosevelt is back and typing away for me. The Aspen trees have their full leaves now and are shimmering like scales. As I sit out reading in the morning the early plane comes in, white fuselage against the green mountains, I watch it like a prisoner; it is filled with my dreams. The long summer is beginning.

When I think that I know you, you uncommunicative clod, I am thrilled.

. . .

In his September 3 letter, Salter's reference to Into That Darkness *indicates a book by the writer Gitta Sereny, published that year.* The Young Lions *was a novel by Irwin Shaw, concerned with the experiences of soldiers in World War II. It was made into a 1958 film starring Marlon Brando, Montgomery Clift and Dean Martin.*

. . .

September 3
On the way to Paris

Cher Robt,
What makes me feel this is the last time I'll see Europe for a while? Probably the prices. Also the waiter at Kleine Scheidegg who made me think of such gloomy things as *The Young Lions*.

I had a fine companion for a while, a *New Yorker* writer and physicist, Jeremy Bernstein, do you know him? He left for the States yesterday. De Gaulle, he told me, was once informed while looking at a tortoise that they lived a hundred and fifty years. What a pity, the general said, just when you're growing fond of them, they die.

He got $25,000 for a three-part profile/article on Nepal. Art Pays, that's what they should inscribe on its great temples.

I'm going to Bordeaux to open the box that contains my copy-edited and edited manuscript, and to sit down for a week or more of devout work on it. Then I'm going to London: If it's still there. I read some devastating excerpts in the Sunday *Times* of a book that's coming out Sept. 8th called *Into That Darkness*. It's about Treblinka.

Among all the billions, do you think our voices will ever be heard? The vineyards (around Martigny) are beautiful. One is seduced and battered in turn. The result is presumably wisdom. Wisdom! We are clinging to life like lizards.

. . .

"Mme. Cartier-Bresson" is a reference to the wife of Henri Cartier-Bresson, who was a highly influential photographer, often cited as the father of photojournalism.

. . .

September 18
London

Dear Robt,
The soft sound of morning newspapers being turned and the loose coughs of elderly Englishmen. Smoked haddock for breakfast. Tea. On the television, endless civilized commentary on the three parties and the imminent general election. On the sea, dazzling sunshine.

Mme. Cartier-Bresson, who was under the misapprehension that I might be buying her country house, told me about a very nice hotel in Bordeaux in which they once stayed. It was on a small square, facing a church. She'd forgotten the name. By the wildest chance, I stumbled upon it. Marvelous, old hotel. Rough sheets. Huge rooms and baths. Fleas. Across the way they were restoring or repairing the church. At six in the morning they arrived on motorbikes and began breaking glass.

I tried to find Steven Schneider but couldn't. No one at the Bordeaux Wine Syndicate knew of him, nor did the Americans or English in the business that I asked. He wasn't in the telephone book. In any event I was off in Bergerac, Arcachon, and touring the vineyards. Bordeaux is very fine. Quiet, provincial. How I wish I spoke better French.

Have only done 70 pages of the 490 I must do in the manuscript. It's not only the work, it's the anger which surges up. Paragraphs, phrases, adjectives, everything called into question. Two editors, one set of marks in plain pencil, the other in blue. Sometimes they argue with each other in the margin. It will be a stronger book, pruned, treated as if it were an orphan.

Gide prescribed light food and cool temperatures for writing, plus reading a few lines of the classics to set one right before beginning. For this last purpose I am using Virginia Woolf and Mandelstam. English books are so beautiful and so inexpensive, it seems. The French have about twenty words for a woman's behind, it was brought up at dinner a few nights ago. They began to recite them. I could only think of four or five in English. Impoverishment. It depends on what's important to you, they said.

There's a series of books on writers, I don't know if you've seen them. Lots of illustrations, photographs, a kind of biography and discussion of the times. William Sansom did the most recent one, on Proust. There are others, on Wilde, Conrad, Hugo, everyone. Well, not quite everyone. In Père Lachaise there is an incredible, overwhelming winged being, like an Assyrian god in bas-relief, feathers of stone that seem numberless, on [Oscar] Wilde's gravestone. It's huge. Someone has knocked off the penis and balls. In a small, graveled plot like a garden, Molière and La Fontaine are side by side...

The beach here is stones, murderous to walk upon. I have holes in my shoes. I'm ready, I think, to come home.

Did you know that a quack named Dr. Russell who had his patients drink seawater for diseases of the glands established modern Brighton (circa 1750)?

I've missed you.

1975 A Time of Uncertainty and Unease

Salter got divorced in 1975, the same year he published a novel about the dissolution of a marriage. The coincidence is notable, but given his reticence on such matters in Burning the Days*, it is difficult to imagine him performing so naked an act of transcription in* Light Years*. In fact, he has said that he wanted to demonstrate certain attitudes toward living, among them that marriage lasts too long. "Perhaps I was thinking of my own," he told* The Paris Review *in their Art of Fiction series. The reviews for* Light Years *were mixed. The critic Anatole Broyard offered a particularly nasty take, though Salter was "more puzzled by it than anything." George Weidenfeld is, today, Sir Arthur George Weidenfeld. He founded the publishing house Weidenfeld & Nicolson, along with Harold Nicolson. Salter was also writing for magazines at the time, including a piece on the writer Antonia Fraser, and later one on Nabokov, both for* People*, hard as it is to imagine the* People *of today publishing anything like a piece on Nabokov. Phelps was less involved with journalism, having grown weary of writing to order. Instead he taught at the New School and edited the writer Glenway Wescott's journals for a book that became* Continual Lessons*. Also worth noting, he seemed cautiously optimistic about the medications he was taking for Parkinson's.*

. . .

Lady Antonia Fraser is a writer of both history and fiction and the widow of Harold Pinter.

. . .

January 15
Paris

Cher Robert,
Nothing but difficulties here, trembling on the disastrous. Nabokov claims to be sick—I sent him a telegram saying "Suddenly I am not feeling very well myself . . . "—and Graham Greene has seen a copy of *People* and decided it is not suitable, this cheap little rag, for someone of his stature. So it's like Antonia Fraser's story (she was marvelous) of going to Irwin Shaw's in Klosters for dinner and being told at the door that the time had been changed, or something, and the table was full. She and Geo. Weidenfeld were speechless with anger. I'm a bit sore myself.

Bergman has agreed to see me, but he would like to see me on the 17th of February. I'll probably be back in New York this weekend.

It's like summer here. People bicycling. Beautiful clothes. France is like a beast with paralyzed hind legs, seriously injured, but the head goes on eating vigorously.

How is Glenway?

I'm a little down.

. . .

Dame Maggie Smith is an English actress. She has earned two Academy Awards, one for her work in The Prime of Miss Jean Brody *and one for* California Suite. *Fernand Crommelynck was a Belgian playwright, known for works such as* The Magnificent Cuckold *and* Mad for Love.

. . .

February 12
Chamonix

Dear Robert,
I wrote to Glenway to see if he won't give something to Random House. It could be a big help depending on what he writes, if he does. Your story about his wandering off into reminiscences when he was writing

about a book he genuinely liked hasn't made me confident. The first piece in *People* will be in next week's issue. They called me last night to inform me that Antonia's current boyfriend, Robert Stephens, had his front teeth knocked out by Maggie Smith, his ex-wife or ex-wife-to-be, and shouldn't there be something about Stephens in the article so they wouldn't appear to be too head-in-the-sand about Antonia Fraser's notoriety? I knew about Stephens of course, it was in the newspapers while I was in London, but they were bleating that there had to be some mention, and so they read me their proposed addition, a banal parenthesis about "Current gossip is . . . " Following the custom to which you introduced me, I had an icy martini in hand, virtually consumed by then, and I can't think over the telephone anyway, so I had nothing to suggest that would improve the vulgarity. Let it be, I finally said. They had already, also on the phone last week, inserted several paralyzing sentences about her biographer father and mother and novel-writing sister and historian brother. It's all just trivia but these additions do create a pall . . .

I'm supposed to be starting the Nabokov, but I'm waiting for a couple of books from the Gotham, one a *Lolita* annotated by an ex-student, I suppose more properly a former student of Nabokov's named Alfred Appel, Jr., who also wrote something called the *Dark Cinema of Vladimir Nabokov*. Also something called *Strong Opinions*. At least two of these unquestionably are lying in your hallway atop stacks of *Oggi* and *Paris Match*. You've finished the Léautaud?

From Ed. R. Hamilton, Bookseller, I've ordered several copies of *The Literary Life* to put away fresh for giving to someone this next Christmas or any. It's a quarter of a century since you stopped. Isn't it time for 1950–1975? I suppose not. One must have some distance. But you can put it on your calendar to do in the '80s or early '90s.

I'm reading a play of [Fernand] Crommelynck's which is dedicated as follows:

TO THE GREAT BERTHE BADY
WHO BEFORE SHE WAS A PRINCESS DE GROULINGEN

DRUNKEN WITH LOVE
TREMULOUS WITH DESPAIR
GAVE HER FAITH
TO THIS IMAGE
OF AN AGE
WITHOUT FAITH

The play is called *Les Amants Puérils*. Beyond that I know nothing.

Nabokov or Mme. Nabokov, it's hard to separate them in terms of who is saying things, is refusing to allow the photographer to come and do pictures to go with the article. There has been an exchange of half a dozen cables. Nabokov now cagily saying he will allow the photographer if the interview piece is submitted to him for approval. Fortunately, it's *Time*'s inviolable policy not to do this. This was communicated to him. For the moment, silence.

. . .

Kenneth Clark was an English art historian. He served as director of the National Gallery and published a number of volumes of history and criticism during his lifetime. Phelps refers to la baronne de R. in his February 16 letter, a reference to Bethasbée de Rothschild. She was a noted philanthropist and a member of the Rothschild banking family.

. . .

February 16
New York

Cher maître,

Yesterday's mail contained a glassine-windowed envelope from what appeared to be a French travel agency or hotel chain. Along with a couple of other pieces of "junk" mail, I popped it into the waste basket. That was a little before noon. Half an hour before martini time (5 sharp), I was drowsing at the desk, half-listening to *Das Rheingold*, bored with scissoring up *père* Jouhandeau, wishing the telephone would ring. I glanced down at the wastebasket and happened to remember that years ago I almost threw out a check from *Harper's Bazaar* by neglecting to open an envelope. So without curiosity, merely for the form, I reached down and recovered a flier from the NYC Ballet, an announcement for some Soho opening, and the windowed envelope from France, oddly bearing an American airmail stamp. I opened it and pow!

I have been eagerly on the lookout for your first piece in *People* and shall be in line at the newsstand Tuesday morning. The editorial inserts are outrageous but there is nothing one can do. In the years I wrote for Wm. Buckley, one of his editors had me use the word "hogwash"—in a particularly brutal, corny context—and I haven't gotten over it yet . . .

I'll speak earnestly to Glenway about the blurb. He's been euphoric in the past few weeks, after a bad fortnight of despair. One morning he phoned about seven, saying he was sitting naked next to an open oven, shivering and reading three notebooks on Alfred Kinsey. But his bodily health is splendid and he has a new 29-year-old lover; and Friday afternoon he walked me around Manhattan from one until five, at which time I was exhausted and he was still bouncing. The only difficulty about the blurb is the fact that Glenway gave his copy of the proofs to *la baronne de R.* and is, I suspect, embarrassed to ask Random House for another. But I'll prod him, and then hope he says something that can be used.

No news. I paste and snip alternately at Jouhandeau (a sort of "autobiographical" collage à la *Earthly Paradise*) and Volume III of Glenway's *journal composé* (called *Continual Lessons*, after Walt Whitman). This earns my rent and Tanqueray. Otherwise—after two mortal years—I am trying to write some pages of my own. My paw seems to quiver less, and I continue to have faith in my Armenian neurologist and to take my daily dose of 10 L-Dopa pills and 2 Symmetrels. Astrologically, there are curious and unprecedented changes due in the next year or two. I await them reverently.

My New School writing workshop has begun again but so far the class includes neither beauties nor geniuses, only sturdy little egos. Becki's hepatitis seems to have run its course, winding up with a capricious flurry of flu. She, too, has resumed teaching, and the paintings for her April show at Poindexter are ready. Otherwise she reads Kenneth Clark's autobiography and sleeps through her daily quota of television. (Though both of us stayed awake through last night's rerun of *Downhill Racer*, which remains as good as ever. Redford is a fool not to put you on retainer).

Apart from dozens of volumes of Jouhandeau, I've read almost nothing this calendar year. Gone are the days when I browsed dreamily with my Garzanti dictionary and volumes of Pavese, Gadda, Montale, et al. Roger Straus gave me the 2-volume biography of Emily Dickinson but I haven't even taken it out of its slipcase yet. I did read Dorothea Straus's memoir portraits (*Showcases*), but that was in the line of duty. And the only film I've seen for months was Louis Malle's *Lacombe, Lucien*—which I loved. (You and he are Bresson's best "sons," I think).

Becki wants to go to Venice in August (the only time we can get away this year). Puddy pointedly leaves the room whenever the subject is mentioned . . . I met a very handsome corgi the other day: the most intelligent face—furred or otherwise—I've encountered for months.

February 20
New York

Mon fils,

I have fifteen minutes before I have to leave for my New School writing workshop, in which I shall discuss your Fraser piece. In spite of the inserted paragraph, it's very good—watchful, alacritous, professional, and the final paragraph ("It is Friday . . . ") is *echt* Salter, worthy of your signature. The Carlyle quotation is nifty and apt and the nipper (last line) graceful and tidy. You have a various future.

But how—what?—ordained that the same issue should contain a photograph of our Glenway. The same morning it appeared on my local newsstand, G. phoned to read me your letter and his reply. This morning he called to ascertain your Aspen address and read me a preposterous note from Fox's secretary apropos of the second set of page proofs of *Light Years*. The underlings in publishing should be fed to computers LIVE.

Anyway, he'll write the squib, and let us pray it's usable. He's eager to meet you again and charges me to arrange this, so please remind me when you're in Manhattan again to haul Glenway up our 74 steps.

Yesterday I received Volume XXI of père Jouhandeau's *journaliets*. He sent it with an inscription, "*Où en sommes-nous?*"—"Where the hell are we?" It covers the months from July 1966 to February 1967 . . .

Now off to class. I have a well-iced martini in a thermos bottle. It will look like harmless Sprite when I pour it out.

April 11
And bloody cold, snow everywhere, the water frozen in the mornings

Dearest Robert,

Yes, I am hanging on like a bulldog, I think at last an agreement is about to be signed on a film for Redford—at least he called me the other day and said, let's go . . .

We must talk over summer plans. If I do sign, it will include a trip to Europe. Perhaps we can go at the same time. The work there will be easy for me: listening to taciturn mountaineers talk about their climbs, looking at some of their films, seeing the Turner exhibition if it's still on, perhaps a dash to the sea.

I would like to move the furniture around in my life. It's such a mess the way it is. I had to go to Los Angeles last week to see the movie that might have been standing in our way (*The Eiger Sanction*, not yet released). Suddenly I found myself happy. The smell of oranges in the air, the somewhat melancholy stretches of the city looking like the '30s, the wonderful Hispanic names, the damned good hotel—oh, those days I used to frequent the St. Regis and have lunches put on the bill!

I'm going to read Brendan Gill's book [*Ways of Loving*]. I'm dutifully plodding through Harvey Swados's [*Celebration*]. Dear man. He once confessed to me, an afternoon in France: I have every quality of genius except talent.

In a restaurant in Hollywood (Joe Allen's) there was N.(!) and a woman at the next table named Dascha Auerbach Stuart whom I hadn't seen for years. She remembered me as a firebrand, she said, "Tell me, have you changed your ideas since then?"

"I don't know," I said, "What were they?"

Can we see Glenway? He gave Fox a very nice quote, a bit too crammed with adjectives (don't tell him that, please) as a result, I think, of Fox's artless urging (They did it on the phone, I'm told).

. . .

"M. Léautaud" is a reference to the French writer Paul Léautaud, another author whose work was seldom translated into English and a favorite of Phelps. Léautaud was a rather eccentric figure. He never married and lived with as many as fifty animals in his house at times. His love life was active and often troublesome all the same, as evidenced in his journals, which cover the whole of his adult life.

. . .

May 6
Aspen

Mon vieux,
Five o'clock and in a fine glass the faint cracking of ice that swims in Gordon's gin. I would like a finer gin, the superb gin that the king's son bears . . . but I am still waiting for the first check, no more than a blown leaf from the high bowers of Hollywood but all the world to me. I wrote to Molly McKaughan (of *The Paris Review*, as if you didn't know) mysterious lines of praise of you intermixed with references to M. Léautaud. Has she rung? Ah, but you were grand to me, almost pleading for a story and here I am getting drunk and too busy anyway to write one. A story, I find, is like a vow to lose twenty pounds. One must gather every resource, one must prepare for a struggle of weeks, even months, and every moment the danger of giving up, giving in. I have been trying to write a certain story for five years. It is called "The Ace of Aces" or sometimes "Fallen Aces" and then again "Amiable Champions" and I know what it is, I know exactly what it is but like the name of someone or someplace it is floating just out of reach. I can

see everything except the actual lines. I would like to retire and write. And right! I should say.

The other evening a general, a real general, anyway once a real general with four stars and a chest full of colored ribbons, once a general always a general, it is a rank like governor or maestro—anyway a general came by. We were drinking. Whatever happened to that lady who didn't think she could get home? he asked. (Yvonne, who was drunk at a party last summer and who is dangerous at the wheel under the best of conditions). What was her name? he said. I saw her just the other day in New York, I said, she's ravishing. Later, after dinner, I was offered a strange drink by his new wife. Here, she said, have you ever tried it? He's tried everything, the general said. I knew then that my life was not wasted.

Karyl Roosevelt is working at the Guggenheim Foundation on 10th(?) Street, a few doors away, for two anthropologists (?) named Tiger and Fox. This is not code. I expect to be in New York at the end of the month. What have you determined about Europe? Please try and be serious.

June 12
Aspen

Dear Robt,
I am eating coffee toffee and recovering from the trials of New York. Our pony ran away last night, knocking down or chewing through some corral rails to do it. She's back now, contentedly grazing in the shade of the cottonwood. Tremendously intelligent eyes this girl has, I cannot look into them without musing on reincarnation. Carne, carnal, carnate, I love that word.

What's Ned Rorem's address? I must send him a book.

One of the great institutions of Aspen is about to vanish: the P.O. Box. Home delivery is beginning next month. Not only will there be no reason for me to distractedly bicycle into town every noon, I have to put up a mailbox. In principle that might seem easy, but there are the huge winter drifts to plan for . . .

Why is it so difficult to assemble those things that really matter in life and to dwell among them only? I am referring to certain landscapes, persons, beasts, books, rooms, meteorological conditions, fruits. In fact, I insist on it.

. . .

Salter's complaints here stem from the critic Anatole Broyard's review of Light Years. *Broyard characterized the book as "about the crisis of marriage," and added, "is there any other kind of novel?" He also called the couple at the heart of the book "insulting to our patience and our expectations."*

. . .

June 30
Aspen

Yes, Nedra, Viri, Arnaud, Ursula, and Anatole.

Your colleague is very dense. He cannot even read properly. The line he attributed to Nedra is actually Mrs. Reinhart's and, of course, has nothing to do really with Celine.

The other line, "I adore biography" is spoken by a simpering and effeminate man . . .

You've sent me Ned's address. Please, amigo, put it on a postcard. We are having Nebraska temperatures, 95° and higher. Many of the tropical suits worn by distinguished visitors are wilting.

What's your opinion of the piece in *People*? Is it as foolish as it makes me feel?

Speak to me, this is a time of uncertainty and unease. That poor man who was drunk in your place that night. Did he survive? Will we?

July 15
New York

Dear, dear Jim,

Peter Deane arrived from Boston Sunday, bearing a copy of Broyard's review, and then yesterday your own Xerox copy came.

I don't know what to say. I'm horrified, of course. The review is imperceptive and unjust, missing or misrepresenting your intentions entirely. But worse, it is mean, snide, snotty (Why Rome? Because it's baroque, dummy!) in a degree I cannot understand. If I am to believe Broyard when he tells me how much *A Sport and a Pastime* meant to him, then why such a vicious show of hostility to the same author's next book? Why not sympathy, respect, reverence? Even if *Light Years* disappoints him, it is by a writer he has been awed by. Why not token courtesy? Why make scornful fun of something patently serious by someone he respects?

The only reason I can think of is the obvious one. Broyard himself is a novelist manqué, and the kind of novel you have written in *A Sport* and *Light Years* ("Yes of course it's about the crisis of marriage. Is there any other kind of novel?") is the kind Broyard would have written, had his creative powers been robust enough, or fluent enough, or simply ample enough.

But I don't give a damn about Broyard's why or wherefore. I'm ashamed for him. As for you, I wish I could clasp your hand, or hold you in my arms for a minute, and somehow make you feel the love and tenderness and empathy I have for you, both as a writer I envy and revere above any other contemporary, and as a man and a friend and a confrere. Bless you. *Light Years* is a beautiful vision, exquisitely embodied in sentences that are all your own, and full of *choses vues* that only James Salter has ever shown me. I love your book—your books—your films.

Peter was as angry as I. He had asked *The Boston Globe* to let him do a review, but one was already in the works, by someone called Margaret Manning. It came out last week and found your book "dazzling."

This is only a hasty note, to apologize for having seemed to neglect writing you so flagrantly all this spring. I have been having problems and self-absorptions and fits of spleen. And this month—rightly your month—has been clotted with teaching and hours of daily commuting. More Friday. Meantime a bearhug—three bearhugs, one from Becki, one from Peter, one from me.

July 19
Aspen

Dear Robert,
I have your loving letter. Don't be alarmed by that review. I'm more puzzled by it than anything else. Margaret Manning is the book editor of the *Globe* and wife to the editor of the *Atlantic*. I'm told she's well-regarded. Her review is the exact opposite of Broyard's. Anyway they are not the only readers, they are the paid readers.

I think of you always. I speak of you always. You don't have to write. In fact, a letter is like a poem, it leaps into life and shows very clearly the marks, perhaps I should say thumbprints, of an unwilling or unready composer.

I'm reading *Decline and Fall*. I was laughing aloud at the airport (going to Denver). People were leaning forward to be able to see the title of the book. I love Waugh for being an arch-conservative, that is for being himself and unlike anyone else.

New York must be absolute chaos. Of course, you needn't read the papers, I suppose, except *The Village Voice*, which comes here, is like last letters from Stalingrad. I can't read it without weeping.

. . .

Phelps didn't travel as frequently as Salter did, but he did spend time in England in 1975. A fuller account of his trip can be found in his September 6 letter.

. . .

August 1
London

Of course no good book was ever written here since the place itself is too studied, eloquent, staged, self-conscious. But it is beautiful, even in a drought, and the Tower view of the Weald of Kent is sovereign. Do you know a Knightsbridge pub called the Grenadier? That's where we'll have out first London pint of bitter together. If only that day were to be today!

August 4
Aspen

Chers voyageurs,
Immense heat has seized the east of the nation. Weather goes from west to east, you will probably soon experience or are now having one of those irregular periods when Chaleur strikes Albion and the English go mad, there are dog bites, acts of unspeakable violence and irrationality, etc, and the surly English temper rushes forth . . .

You are in the land of Anthony Blond [the English publisher and writer], bless you. Have a bit of veal and ham pie for me, with English mustard, and if you have time, a Dover sole at Wheeler's in Duke of York Street, you probably know it, eight feet wide, I think the only place to sit there is at the downstairs bar. If the pound keeps falling, perhaps it will all come to less than $10.

I'm told that Random House has fired a broadside and that a handsome ad appeared in today's *NY Times* (why Monday, I wonder?). I was also told that sales last week were 648 copies! Which for me is phenomenal, even miraculous.

I had a letter, a note really, from Graham Greene. He cited certain pages as "masterly." Upon looking them up, I found they were all decidedly Greene-like, pages he, himself, might have written. Still, it was very nice. He asked if I had an English publisher. No, but I have some Peel shoes.

My hands are full of splinters. I think of you as being in the midst of inimitable life.

August 14
Aspen
Storms

Robert, my lad,
I was thinking of you yesterday early in the morning, sitting in a bath and soaking my legs in nice, hot water, the windows open and a grey, rainy sky outside. Also reading [Robert] Craft's *Stravinsky*, both because you commended it to me and because even if you hadn't, it reminds me

of you. I like Stravinsky's music, yes, sometimes enormously, but more than that I like the idea of life he represents. There's a lot of Auden in it, as you know.

Just back from Jackson Hole, Wyo. The drive there is absolutely trans-Siberian in length, a day and a half each way, but through ravishing country. For at least a hundred miles north of Rock Springs (Wyo.) there is nothing on either side but the country that existed when the Indians had it and the earliest trappers and explorers appeared (in the 1800s). Not a house, barely a road, not a telephone pole. One is absolutely thrilled that it exists. Finally there are a couple of isolated farming towns and then the civilization in the vast area south of Jackson Hole.

In Farson, which was one of the little towns, I stopped at the Post Office–General Store. There had been a sign of nearing an historical marker half a mile back.

"Where's the historical marker?" I asked.

The old woman gestured out the window. Across the road was a small, stone obelisk.

"It's right there," she said.

"Ah. What does it say?"

"I don't know," she replied.

I went to Jackson to talk to some climbers. Les Grands Tetons are imposing, they rise abruptly from the ranch meadows, though what made the crazed French trappers dream they resembled breasts is difficult to know.

The best news I've had is that my book is selling, modestly, it's true, but by my standards, not bad, 750, 270, and 523 copies each of the past three weeks respectively, 6,300 so far.

I had a very kind letter Ned Rorem sent to Joe Fox forwarded to me, in fact, a wonderful letter, and also a letter of condolences and encouragement from Saul Bellow, he's probably too furious now to have done it, the daily *Times* review of his new book is awful, I'm told, as is *The Village Voice*'s and, it is said, the forthcoming *Sunday Times*. It's very sad though, of course, it won't hurt him in the large sense. It is good to know the game isn't fixed.

The draft of the Greene piece is finished. Today/tomorrow I'm beginning my heart-surgeon script.

How is England?

. . .

Radclyffe Hall was the author of The Well of Loneliness, *a novel notable for its treatment of lesbian themes, particularly as it was published in 1928. It was the subject of lengthy obscenity trials in both the UK and the US.*

. . .

September 6
New York

Dear Jim,
About the time you're reading this—i.e. next Tuesday morning—I shall be lying "etherized upon a table," under the knife, having my 14-year-old rupture repaired. Say a modest prayer for me, and reflect in passing on the strangeness of life: it was October 8, 1961, lugging a monstrous suitcase full of Ned Rorem's mss. and diaries, that the original split occurred.

London was above all civil; humane, courteous, unclamorous, a *machine à vivre*. It was also brimming with Arabs, the ladies in strict purdah and the gentlemen reputed, with their new wealth, to be planning to erect a mosque in Regent's Park; scattered with excellent Italian restaurants; cosy with pubs; and as ever, wonderful simply to walk in (that's why Henry James lived there, I'm sure). We had a service flat in Queens Gate and after the first torrid days, the most exquisite weather I can remember anywhere. For the first time in my life, I was a tourist. I visited Jane Austen's Bath, Henry James's Rye, E. M. Forster's Cambridge (where, to my consternation, the lodge porter at King's College did not know who Forster was), Auden's Oxford, and one misty afternoon, even went up to Highgate in search of Radclyffe Hall's grave. (It's been temporarily closed, due to the grilled entrance having been broken down by fervent ladies. But George Eliot and Karl Marx are just across the lane, so the visit was not in vain).

My new literary love appears to be Ivy Compton-Burnett. At Foyle's, I bought 14 of her 19 books (she shrewdly left her publisher fifteen thousand pounds to keep them all in print), and I reverently passed her apartment in Cornwall Gardens (now the embassy of the Dominican Republic) every day. She requires absolute concentration, but almost every page is like a brand on the memory. She is ruthlessly unsentimental, fiercely true to egotistical side of human nature, and at the same time, funny. She is exhausting to read, but the flavor of her mind is unique: like a hypnotized child, she speaks the unspoken, the unspeakable, and it's a constant, curious shock. I'm taking her to the hospital with me.

Oh yes, I paid a dutiful call on Miss [Brigid] Brophy, and was presented to her friend Miss Duffy, her consort Mr. Levey, her 15-year-old daughter Kate, her daughter's 17-year-old Canadian boyfriend Craig, and some 15 pigeons. Brigid does indeed wear green nail polish. And she likes her gin un-iced and straight.

Driving through Somersetshire, prowling the Brighton waterfront, sitting on the great lawns of Wilton House, and especially sipping white wine in a dear pub called the King's Head and Eight Bells (next door to Carlyle Mansions, where Henry James died), I thought about you, and your lambent book, and we talked about our lives and aspirations. How I wish you had been there! "Another time," as Auden said. Perhaps next year. But next spring, what if we were in Venice? Or even in London again? Do you know the tiny pub in Wilton Row called the Grenadier? And I found a restaurant called Casa Portelli, and another in Gloucester Road called the Gondoliere which are both unlisted in those lousy guidebooks and both sterling. And there's a pub in Greenwich called the Trafalgar which is heavenly on Sundays, with the Thames flowing by and a pint of bitter and some cold smoked turkey and salad, and Wren's magnificent naval school next door.

How are you deep down inside? Very angry about the book? And the script about heart-surgery? I'll be back from the hospital about the 15th and hope to find an envelope from Aspen.

. . .

The film Salter was working on, temporarily known as Heart Beats, *was released in 1981 as* Threshold, *directed by Richard Pearce and starring Donald Sutherland and Jeff Goldblum. "Mankiewicz, père" is a reference to Joseph Mankiewicz, a writer and director whose credits included* All About Eve *and* Cleopatra.

. . .

September 8
Aspen

Dear Robert,
I think of writing to you so many times. Have you gone to France? I went to California and stole a day to drive to the great vineyards in the Napa Valley. What a day! *Fin d'octobre* and the autumn sun, which to me is the sweetest of all, pouring down. A picnic up a little side road, beneath huge and sighing eucalyptus trees, and the voices of young people picking grapes, carried to us from down among the vines. There are some lovely restaurants and at least two ravishing hotels there, both minute and very French in feeling. To give an idea of the pace of life, the restaurants are closed Mon.–Tues.—and sometimes Wed.

I am so happy. It is the happiness of doing what I like to do in a place I like to be—that is, this house. And today it was snowing. Unfortunately, I don't have my old dog. He cries when he sees me and puts his paws up on my leg. Tolstoy once said of Gorky: "He has the nose of a duck—only unhappy and unkind men have a nose like that. Women, too, don't love him, and women are like dogs, they can scent a good man."

This part of growing old is very agreeable, still able to see and hear and sure of oneself and not wanting everything on earth, for a change.

Before me are spread all the notes for an essay on cemeteries I'm supposed to do for *Antaeus*. I still can't find the bit that's supposed to start it, but I'm sure it's in there. The body of the emperor (Napoleon) is contained in six coffins. The innermost is of tin-sheathed iron, the next of mahogany, the third and fourth of lead, the fifth of ebony, the last of oak.

I love details of how people are buried. I love completed lives. Yours is an exception. Yours I would like to continue for ever or at least until people yawn and say, My God, still alive?

I'm writing on the same table on which I eat. Wonderful, warm confusion. Bits of Stilton, stains of tea.

I had a very beautiful letter from Edna O'Brien. Her handwriting is somewhat like Glenway's, or at least the space and structure of the letter. She appears not to remember me, but she is a passionate creature and the dinner we had was probably very dull. Not for me, of course.

The film about the cardiac surgeon, called for the present, temporarily, *Heart Beats*, is finished, needs now only about a week or two on certain things that are to be revised. I think it's quite good. It has some vivid people and vivid in the sense of true rather than merely outrageous or shocking. It remains to be seen if it will be made. But as Mankiewicz, *père*, said: The inescapable fact is that a properly written screenplay has in effect already been directed.

So there you are. Did I tell you that Robt. Ginna has been rewarded for his season in hell by being made chief NY editor for Little, Brown? Of course he still longs to make films, but the world is filled with madmen.

September 10
Aspen

Dear Invalid,
Of course you shall have a letter. You need it, you deserve it. I should be in the hospital myself and at least have an excuse for not having finished this film, although I'm on p. 73 and the worst is surely over. The most fun of writing it is I have a French stencil set for the cardinal numbers and the reward for having finished a page is putting the number on the next one. In the way of all children I sometimes want my reward before having earned it. That's the extent of my wickedness. Some of the script is good. I have no opinions beyond that and as for hope: never. At least I am past that.

As for deep inside, no, I'm not angry. The truth is that things are turning out much as expected. *Light Years* will sell about 10,000 copies, I think. Those who like it, I am grateful for. Those who don't, I pray are misguided. The pair of bad reviews in the *Times* was unfortunate. I thought at least I'd have a split. No, I am confident, probably mistakenly so, and serene.

I never finished the little three cabins from the lumber town that I moved to the hills overlooking a majestic valley of meadows and ranches and beyond it, Mt. Sopris, vast, it seems as Everest. I hadn't the time or enough money. They will winter there, half-complete and perhaps I'll get back to them in the spring.

My wife and I are parting. There are two children still at home which pains me, but I won't be far off, just a few minutes' walk. There is a time to put one's self first, I suppose that's explaining it simply. But also inadequately. I'm moving out next week. The terrible thing is all the books, I'm so tired of picking them up. So I may be silent for a while, adjusting to a new life. A life far closer to the center of me . . .

I love the fall. It's the time of year I have well-being, hope, even a kind of intoxication. I went out and bought a new handle for my ax.

Be well. I think of you always.

J.

We had dinner and then, a few days later, tea with Yvonne. She's about to return to NY. She told a very uncharacteristic story about Leonard being in jail in France. She put on a Molineaux hat and a fur coat and went down to the Sante to see him. She had an old lawyer, he had a white beard. When Leonard was finally released, two weeks later, "we celebrated," she said. 1938.

. . .

Lorenzo Semple is a screenwriter Salter knew from Aspen. He was at the time working on the Dino De Laurentiis-produced film, Hurricane. *He also wrote for the* Batman *TV series of the 1960s, and wrote the scripts for* The Parallax View *and* Three Days of the Condor.

. . .

J.P. Donleavy is the author of The Ginger Man, *originally published by Maurice Girodias as part of the* Traveler's Companion *series for Olympia Press. Many of the books in the series were considered pornographic, and Donleavy resented his inclusion in such company. He sued Girodias and was eventually able to buy Olympia Press at its bankruptcy auction. Diana and Lionel Trilling were literary critics, writers, and members of the New York Intellectuals. They were married for forty-five years, until Lionel Trilling's death in 1975.*

. . .

November 19
Aspen

Dear Robt.,
Are you back from France? I read J. P. Donleavy's interview in *The Paris Review* today. When people speak, they do make fools of themselves.

I also went to Diana Trilling. When they were with me, she was much stronger than Lionel. Perhaps it was that I was in awe of him, and I was. He had black circles under his eyes and didn't look well. This is, to a degree, in retrospect. After all, Diana looked a bit worn herself.

Today an essay, an article really, called "Cemeteries" went off to *Antaeus*. I am essentially uneducated. I shouldn't get into these things. Organizing hard, that is to say, critical knowledge, is beyond me. If I want to read an essay called "Cemeteries," I want it written by Ortega y Gasset or Borges with the wisdom of vast libraries and decades of patient discourse.

That was written last night, somewhat exhaustedly. This morning, all is different. A pure snow is falling, silence everywhere. A fire burning, my dog asleep on the bed and a symphony on the record player.

I'm to meet Redford tomorrow either here or in Denver. These will be the final discussions. Then I must sit down and write the film. Over the holidays, the arrival of visitors, the first days of bitter cold.

I wanted to use something from Auden's "In Memory of W. B. Yeats" but I couldn't find the proper phrase or line. Instead I read the whole of *Our Lady of the Flowers* again to make an opening paragraph. What has that to do with cemeteries? Ah, well . . .

I don't think I'm coming to New York, at least there are no plans. I have an old display case, oak and glass, in which are glasses, vermouth, plates and Tanqueray gin, and I follow that sacred practice of yours at five o'clock every day.

a las cinco de la tarde
A las cinco de la tarde
A las cinco en punta de la tarde . . .

Apart from all this, I am very content. Of course, the ship is not running exactly right yet, but it's coming along. I particularly like not having to say where I am going or why, and lingering at the bar for half an hour or so if I am inclined. I feel I am opening my wings and unruffling my feathers.

Did I tell you that Robert Ginna, the passionate Life of, is now seated in the chair of chief New York editor for Little, Brown?

I long to see that yellow paper you are fond of typing on and to read bits about Jouhandeau. Night before last we sat here with ice-filled martinis in clear wine-glasses and I read rashers of *Professional Secrets* ("What a great title," he said) to Lorenzo Semple.

. . .

If it seems that Salter knew almost everyone at some point, that's because he did know a great many people and crossed paths with several others. He did not pretend to greater familiarity with these figures than he really had, referring to the publisher Clay Felker, the writer Gail Sheehy, and the former New York City mayor John Lindsay as "the great figures of your city." Also detailed here is a run-in with the daughter of the great film producer Irving Thalberg and the actress Norma Shearer.

. . .

December 20
Aspen

Dear Robt. & Becki,

Bonne noël. Your beautiful card from France was like a scarab and I have the Bresson on the desk to imbue as much as it can the script I am now writing for Robt. R. I'm going to take some photographs of my house and send them to you, this house which I built myself, brought back to life, that is, and with which I am very content.

The great figures of your city are lapping at the edges of this small and stratospheric town. Clay Felker and Gail Sheehy have rented a friend's house a few blocks from here. John Lindsay—does that name ring a bell?—has bought land in Woody Creek, which is sort of a suburb of Aspen. There's a new bookshop here, a really beautiful one, that was opened by Catherine Thalberg, dtr. of Him and Norma Shearer. It's called Explore. She's a violent feminist. We have already bloodied one another. At a party one evening she kept at me about how Nedra had not "achieved" all she might have following her marriage. As a person, that is. She was at a low level of consciousness, etc. Finally I turned to her and said, look, I can't, I don't discuss things in such terms. What terms? If someone says to me, I said, that they have read my book but the exploitation of the proletariat is not sufficiently emphasized in it, I know one thing: we are not talking about literature—and the same thing applies here. You're sick, she said.

Yes, we must find ourselves some time in France. My life will be different next year, how often have I said it. Still, it occasionally comes true.

I'm reading Sybille Bedford's Huxley biography. It's very nice. Long. The temperature drops to 10 below at night here. Enclosed, the galleys for the piece for *Antaeus*. I like the opening.

Be well, as they say. Multiply.

1976–1977 The Reward of Courage

In 1976 Phelps was finishing work on Belles Saisons, *a scrapbook of Colette's life. He also taught at Manhattanville College, though in a letter from later in the year he mentioned his intention to once again begin earning his living by doing something other than teaching. This apparently proved difficult to arrange in short order, for he taught at Manhattanville during 1977 as well. Salter spent part of 1976 in California, in the name of screenwriting, and, later that year, in France and Italy, the latter as part of his research for a piece on the poet Gabriele D'Annunzio. Perhaps most significant, it was during these years that he became deeply involved with his current wife, the playwright Kay Salter, née Eldredge, a fact which is not made entirely clear in his letters.*

1976

. . .

*Phelps's first letter of 1976 demonstrates the breadth of his reading, including references to everyone from the German writer Ernst Jünger (*Storm of Steel*) to T.S. Eliot, to an oblique mention of the writer George Wickes and his book* Americans in Paris.

. . .

January 22
New York

Dear James,
The enclosed, which I clipped for you in Paris, just fell out of a book of Jünger's essays (*Le Contemplateur Solitaire*) which I must have been reading with my *café complet* one morning last November.

The 280-some Colette photographs are finally turned in: now I must finish the captions and something called *a vol d'oiseau*, a chronology of dates, quotations, bits of colored glass, gossip. Earlier this week I prepared a lecture I love, the first of 13 in a series called Americans in Paris I'm giving at Manhattanville this spring. (No, I'm not cribbing from Geo. Wickes's very good book. Our selections differ and my views are fairly daffy). I begin by passing around a 10 franc note bearing Berlioz's picture and then proceed to describe the view from my room 42 at the Hotel du Quai Voltaire. Then I quote Wilder on Americans ("insubmissive, lonely, self-educated and polite") and T. S. Eliot on Paris ("*C'est à Paris que je me coiffe/Casque noir de jemenfoutiste*") and discuss the significance of the front porch, the pony express, the clipper ship, the telegraph and the Pacific Ocean, all American dreams. Then on to Poe, who never lived in, visited, or even glimpsed Paris, yet used it as the setting for the world's first three detective stories. If you've never read "The Murders in the Rue Morgue" (an invented street, by the way), do. If only for one dear, wistful sentence: "Books, indeed, were his sole luxuries, and in Paris these are easily obtained."

I also love Lecture #2, about Gertrude Stein's *Four in America*, with a lovely quote from Cole Porter ("I love Paris in the winter, when it drizzles/I love Paris in the summer, when it sizzles . . . ").

Lest I forget, this is intended to be a letter of introduction for a young tennis instructor who was in one of my writing workshops, who is talented, and who admired *A Sport*. His name is Douglas Gunther and I told him to drop you a postcard and present my respects. I suspect he'd like to glimpse your work table (as I would myself). He won't pester, I'm sure, and anyway, apprentices have certain inalienable rights vis-à-vis masters.

March 7
Dawn in Los Angeles
The parties are over

Dear Robt.,
The end of a week here. I've come with two films written, armed with them I should say, and a producer willing to pick up the tab for the Beverly Wilshire.

I haven't written to you for so long. I've traded houses: mine in Aspen for one on the beach in Venice (this Venice) for the summer. I'd rather be in Maine, but this was the best I could do. I want to write a play, a really good play, the idea which I'd been carrying around with some paper-clips and pennies suddenly became irradiated, I sat down and scribbled madly. Perhaps it will have an Italian word for the title. I've never asked you, are you fond of the theatre? *Basta.*

The films are *Hearts*, of course, and *Solo Faces*. An exhausted Redford, his voice gone, croaked to me that he would read the latter this coming week. He's been buried in the completion of *All the President's Men*, which must be delivered to Warner's this Thursday and has its world premiere about 4 April, I suppose in Washington.

In my pocket is the check for delivering the script. Much more to come if he likes it. I think it's the best film I've ever written. I'll be crushingly disappointed if it's not cherished.

Yesterday a picnic on the beach in the winter sun which does not burn. My jaws hurt from all the drinking these past nights and my eyes burn. The final night always has little sleep.

I broke my shoulder in January. And am tired from these two films back to back. But the obligation is to earn bread, the kind that is baked. I'm reading Maurois' *Balzac*. He wrote 60 pages a day. This great, oaken example shames one. His uncle was guillotined for the murder of a pregnant farm girl.

Your letter is not before me. When does your Colette book come out? Will I see one?

I must bathe.

. . .

Robin Swados is the son of the writer Harvey Swados. He is also a playwright, perhaps best known for A Quiet End, *one of the earliest dramatic treatments of the implications of HIV in America.* Under the Volcano *is a novel by Malcolm Cowley concerned with the drinking and marital problems of a former British consul officer in Mexico.*

. . .

May 4
Aspen

Ah, Robert,
I have thought so much of you, not to mention a letter from Robin Swados. I was reading Simone de Beauvoir's *Coming of Age* a few nights ago and came across pages devoted to Paul Léautaud. When is your *Paris Review* piece coming out? Do you go to Plimpton's parties? Do they ever talk about me?

This winter has been devoted to script writing, I'm glad to see it past. *Solo Faces*, the film written for Redford, was sent off February 23. Probably the best script I've ever written. I have not heard a peep for these two months and more. I've tried to call him twenty times. Nothing. I even hung around Los Angeles for a week hoping to hear from him. No. So when you think of the glamour and ease of film writing, think of this. Unspeakable business. No wonder everyone is corrupted by it. I had hoped to sit down and start a book, I was determined to do one in a year from the day of beginning, but that was predicated on having the film money tucked beneath the mattress. Now I not only can't begin but may have to take another job. I've been talking about rewriting *The Big Sleep* which Faulkner and a girl named Leigh Brackett did in 1946. Famous, stylish film with impenetrable plot. In fact, the director Howard Hawks and the writers wired Chandler to ask him to clarify it, who killed Owen Taylor? they wanted to know. After a while a telegram came back from Chandler: I don't know. This time they want to make it in England for reasons that are typical of what they call the film industry and they wanted a writer with a little class. Of course, class to the film industry is the Pullet Surprise, as the California papers once printed it, or ownership of a three-piece suit. Anyway, they haven't offered anything yet and I'm waiting to see.

Meanwhile I've traded my house here for one in Malibu for July and August. I promised these two *mômes* I still am father to that they could see the ocean this summer and the east coast was simply too far. Also, people from California had seen my house. I had a better arrangement previously, a house right on the beach itself in Venice which is like Soho with drug-crazed undergraduates and actors, larcenous Moors and dissolution in the very air, but the woman who owned it decided suddenly that she couldn't afford to trade, she had to sell the house and by God, she did two weeks later for $235,000. It's still my dream to reach Maine one summer when you are in residence.

If I do get this film job, I'll be coming through New York before the month is out. If not, I don't know what. I can crawl back to *People*. I feel disoriented. I'm even thinking of reading *Under the Volcano*. Are you going back to France? I see Ned won the Pulitzer. That poor Puerto Rican boy, the celebration and all. Please, some news, anything.

June 11
Aspen

Tu me manques.

A year since I've been to New York, and what a year. I thought I might come a month ago, I had agreed to do a new *The Big Sleep* set in England but the money UA offered was absolutely unbelievable, that is to say, miserly, and as Chandler himself observed, one doesn't do films for glory or artistic challenge. So I'm stewing around waiting to do the revisions on Redford's film. The days, the months are just eaten up. I'm to go to Utah to confer with him next week. He was here for a couple of days in late May. One thing I admire very much about you, I said, is how dangerously close you stay to the line between what you might have been and what you are. That interests me, what do you mean by that? he demanded. That's all I can say, I told him. Something there is in me that hates famous men. Envy is what it is.

Light Years is being remaindered. It sold about 7,000 copies. I'm hemming and hawing about starting again, trying to put together a year's money first. That used to be about $7,500, now it's about $20,000. Poor Joe Fox, his youngest son, serving in the navy, was in an auto accident in Perth and is a quadriplegic. I've thought about that almost every day since it's happened. There he lies and here I complain. Across his chest, Joe told me, is a blue line drawn just below the nipples. Beneath that line, he will never feel again.

I'm reading a few books to prepare myself to sit down, among them the famed work of Dr. Mario Praz or as it is sometimes (mis)spelled and I almost prefer, Pratz. *The Romantic Agony*—I've seen it mentioned in so many reviews à la Updike and Steiner. I need you to help me. Half of it is in Italian and French.

There's a house in Uzes, near Avignon, that I can rent for a few months this fall. The fare over is the problem. Well, to work on these things.

What are your plans?

. . .

Phelps mentions Lartigue in his June 19 letter, a reference to Jacques Henri Lartigue, a French photographer. His career spanned much of the twentieth century, though many of his most famous photographs date from his childhood.

. . .

June 19
New York

Dear Jim,
Becki is at Yaddo and has authorized another guest, a composer from St. Louis, to spend the night here. I'm waiting for him to arrive and pick up the keys. It's eleven A.M., Saturday, and humid-hot.

I owe you three letters and would hate you if the situation were reversed. As it is, I am contrite and grateful. The fact is, it gets harder and harder for me even to type legibly. The right paw continues to shake, in spite of an exploratory session of hypnosis last week. Apparently, like the heart, the hand also has its reasons. Sandy Friedman insists it is trying to tell me something, etc. and I believe this but am having translation problems . . .

I'm incoherent today. I have an assignment to write 2,500 words on Lartigue, and I have any number of books and documents to take lumber from, but my spirit seems unwilling. I would have been so eager for such a job five years ago; today I feel uninspired. I suspect that I need to fall in love. My soil is dry and "my thoughts grow like feathers, the dead end of life." The proof is that although I have a hundred things to tell you, my head's a blank.

In one of your letters you ask about *The Paris Review*. I went to a huge *festino* some weeks ago and saw people putting wet glasses down on the pool table's greenery. You are much loved and revered by Molly, Fayette, Plimpton, etc. I promised to arrange 50pp. of Léautaud for the magazine this fall.

I have not yet seen *Light Years* in Marlboro's. When I do I'll buy half a dozen. Get a hundred for your own archives. You'll need them for adoring young ladies in 1995 and for grant applications in the meantime.

Ignore Praz's necrophilic book on the Gothic novelists. He's better on household furnishings.

My plans (you ask). To try to type less erratically than, for instance, here. To try to resume earning a living by other than the academy. To go to Martha's Vineyard for the month of August. To fulfill certain contractual obligations. To write some very short "Postcard" stories.

But what about the Redford script money? Shouldn't that secure you for a year or two?

My son has begun to write verse.

Nectarines are here. And blueberries.

. . .

Salter mentions d'Annunzio's Vittoriale in his October 27 letter. This is a reference to the Vittoriale degli Italiani (Shrine of Italian Victories). It is actually an estate in the town of Gardone Riviera and was home to the poet and political figure Gabriele d'Annunzio from 1922 until his death in 1938.

. . .

October 27
The sun half-up the sky in France

Cher ami,
On the glass-topped table these objects:

a black Cintra ashtray
a bottle of Beefeater gin and one of vermouth
two wineglasses with a little clear liquid still in each
a pair of Zeiss sunglasses
gold earrings
a cut glass ice bucket on a tray and a large spoon
a red toothbrush
a metro ticket stamped "OPERA"
a heap of shell necklaces, very fine, speckled, tan and white
deep beige mascara, the plastic capsule that holds contact lenses
a ladies' wristwatch, black face, band of flat silver mesh
a key from the Hotel Bristol Terminus-Avignon, Room no. 70
and on the floor, fallen over, a pair of high-heeled shoes

There it is, the sum of it. Farewell to England. My daughter is across the hall, she met us here. She speaks French now with the ease, and much of the vocabulary, of a Paris whore. We're off to see the palace of the Popes. Then to Uzes and ratatouille tonight, a fire burning if they haven't nicked the wood. I was very pleased to see the Nobel go to Saul. No one can ever have wanted it more. We have the same birthday, ten or eleven years apart. I can't be sure which; he fibs a little. I've been reading *The Hunchback of Notre Dame*. What energy it fills one with. It's like wind filling out the huge, idle sails of one's life. I'll be in France for 3½ more weeks, one trip planned to d'Annunzio's Vittoriale and numerous strolls through the fields.

. . .

The reference to Chateaubriand in Salter's November 25 letter indicates the French writer, diplomat, and politician François-René de Chateaubriand, the man widely regarded as having founded Romanticism in French literature.

. . .

November 25
Cherbourg

Mon cher,
Last hours, last letter from France. This beautiful country, more beautiful than ever, it seems, or perhaps I am only seeing places I never did before. Among them, on the drive from Uzes, where the Gorges du Tarn with some ravishing little towns, principally Ste. Enimie, and then in the Auvergne, Argentat on the banks of the Dordogne. Also Angoulene and Nantes, Dinan and St. Malo. These last were so appealing I have sworn to come back, perhaps next fall while the days are still warm, say, at the end of September. I'm telling you this so you have enough time to prepare because you must come with me. Chateaubriand is buried facing the sea on the Grand Be, a small outcropping off St. Malo, but the tide was in and we couldn't walk out to it. I will be crushed if you know all these places, I was discovering them for you.

The QE-2 arrives at 7 P.M.—I expect it to look like the Rex in *Amarcord*—and leaves two hours later with silver Porsches from Geneva and Munich loaded on and also me, somewhat worn by journeying up here but still kicking. I hate fellow passengers. A lady at the hotel asked if I was American, I said, "No spikka da Inglis." Still, who else would have a dog, cameras, and a tote bag full of books?

Cherbourg is hideous. I intend to finish a Mishima biography and

The Hunchback of Notre Dame during the crossing. Thanksgiving day. What a day for departure! In the bicentennial year!

We went to Lago di Garda to see d'Annunzio's house-museum-mausoleum. What a Smithsonian he lived in and what images the little poet had of himself! His signature was bigger than he was. His cock must have been very big, too, although in a fine exhibition of photographs that was on, there are pictures of a number of the (then) celebrated women in his life and they are not the Ziegfeld girls. It's always more glorious reading about these things, although in *La Presse* this morning was a photo of Louise de Vilmorin's sister at Malraux's funeral, in black, what a fine, aristocratic face. They are toppling, Robert, they are toppling. Soon we will be in the front row. New York on the 30th.

1977

. . .

Philip Barry was an American playwright best known for The Philadelphia Story, *which was made into a film starring Katharine Hepburn, Cary Grant, and Jimmy Stewart. Juan Trippe was the founder of Pan American World Airways.*

. . .

January 25
Aspen

Dear Robert,
Your Garzanti has never danced like this. It must think the Day of Judgment is here. This d'Annunzio will ruin me, I like it so much. I wish there were more photographs. The biographers are so poor. He needs someone with a scalpel, no sense of envy, and an executioner's sense of pity . . . I have a few more books to read. I should begin writing next week. My ambition is to finish this.

I'll be in New York towards the end of February. I have a contract—unheard of!—to do a book, for Robt. Ginna and Little, Brown. Random House was bidding on it, too. I'll tell you about it when I see you. Your sister-in-law was so nice to me that day in the torrential rain. I feel I should send her some little gift, won't you suggest something?

Apart from this, little, except I've been to Samoa. Lorenzo Semple had to go down on business for de Laurentiis and insisted I go along. His aunt—I didn't learn this until the last moment—Philip Barry's widow, she's eighty! came along. I hope my eyes are that open at eighty. She swam every morning at seven, worked all day, traveled, talked, and drank like a publisher. She goes to Venice every summer, I expect she's gone to Europe every year of her life. She expects a certain level of service. When they weren't giving it to her on the airplane, she threatened to call her friend, Juan Trippe, in Hawaii.

Samoa is unfrequented, almost unspoiled. It's like Hawaii in 1905. We climbed through an immense teak and breadfruit forest to reach R. L. Stevenson's grave, on top of a mountain overlooking the harbor, the town, and the most beautiful green land. Their name for him is Tusitala, the teller of tales.

. . .

Nadia Boulanger was a French composer and conductor, and, in fact, the first woman to conduct a major American symphony orchestra. Cynthia Merman was an editor who worked with Howard Zinn, among others.

. . .

February 9
New York

Dear James-O,

This has turned out to be another one of those semesters in which I hustle me out to Manhattanville College two days a week *pour*, as Madame G. once said, *chauffer mon four*. My days are Tuesday and Friday.

Donc, the 22nd being a Tuesday, I won't be here until about 5pm. But anytime after that, please arrive for an arctic martini, tropical talk, temperate plans for St. Malo, etc.

And, speaking of geographical matters, no sentence I can remember, including several majestic ones from *Moby Dick*, quite exceeds in Seven-League-Booterie, the following, from page 2 of your January 25th letter: "Apart from this, little, except that I've been to Samoa . . . "

Neddy Rorem was here yesterday, to borrow "some novels." The latest (7th, I think) volume of his journal was rejected by Simon & Schuster, so our redoubtable hero has decided to write a novel . . . moreover, "in April, when it's warm enough on Nantucket." I recommended *Prater Violet*, *A Sport and a Pastime*, *The Pilgrim Hawk*, *The Good Soldier*, and *The End of the Affair* as models.

Broke. I haven't been this broke for years. Hence Manhattanville; hence dinner this evening with my agent; hence evenings checking a translation of Geo. Sand's memoirs; hence an angrily aspen-like right paw. But Becki's rich and Puddy, though almost old as blessed Nadia Boulanger (who will be 90 in September), is good-looking.

I had a genial tea with Ms. Karyl Roosevelt *et son ami* (*ou peut-être seulement un ami*) the other day and found her exceptionally good company. Maybe we should take her with us to the Oyster Bar.

Have you seen a copy of the new magazine *Quest*? I don't know if it's out yet, but someone brought around a make-ready. Its editors aspire to the "literary quality of *The New Yorker*" (I think it was), the photographic enterprise of *Life* (*mettons*) and the production polish of the *National Geographic*. It is concerned with "achievement." More important, it pays 50 cents (and up) per word. I think we should interview Robert Wilson about his para-theatrical *Einstein on the Beach* and earn our airfare to Parigi.

I owe you half a dozen decent letters. But . . . *mais tu comprends* I have to shave, shower, shampoo and get on uptown. I have to make Cynthia Merman's horoscope. I have to think of something to say at

Anaís Nin's memorial service next week (I'm scheduled for 3 minutes). I have to type a note to Glenway's sister-in-law who has invited me to a concert of ancient musical instruments.

April 17
Aspen

Cher ami,
Bits of dry grass in my hair and a glass of Tanqueray near my hand, I've been working all day out of doors, what a wonderful feeling and the smell of this gin: sublime. Going out for dinner in a few minutes. It's like a town in the path of an enemy advance, almost all the restaurants are closed, the streets are deserted. I just heard that I'll have to rewrite my cardiac surgeon film for the third time without any pay—this time like the other two because how can we afford not to, now that so much work has gone into it already; irrefutable, and there's something in me that acquiesces immediately to the foolish. If making movies is, as everyone agrees, a case of iron determination, perhaps we'll make this one. It is awfully good, although it's becoming more and more vivid, as Scobie would say, with each revision. My friend, Chris Mankiewicz, after years in the wilderness has finally made it in, he's been appointed as head of Columbia Pictures in New York, not the top job but still comfortable. I don't know whether this will help me at all, the nature of the business is that memories are extremely short and even worse, I lent him money, but perhaps this will be an exception. And after all, what do I expect aside from gossip and an occasional meal in an expensive restaurant when I'm in town?

I've been expecting a letter telling me yes, we will sail for France. What's happened? I'm almost definitely going in June, as I said, to lie at the foot of the Dru(s) for a couple of weeks in a tent and make notes. Next week I'm driving to Yosemite to see certain climbers (not social). *Quest*, read Molly McKaughan, is giving me angst about the d'Annunzio piece. Too long. I've cut a thousand words and written some new things for it (a thousand words cut including the new additions) and I'm still waiting to hear that they'll accept it. They sent me a check but I haven't cashed it. If they say they want to cut more, I want to be able to withdraw the article. Of course, who else would take it, but I don't care. Perhaps Plimpton will or perhaps *Antaeus*. If not, there's always the *Aspen Anthology*, no payment other than two free copies for the contributors, but think, my dear, of the glory! Let me hear from you.

. . .

Phelps mentions "La Petite Dame's *second volume on Gide," a reference to a work by Maria van Rysselberghe, the mother of André Gide's daughter. The books were titled* Cahiers de la Petite Dame 1918-1945.

. . .

April 21
New York

Caro Giacomo,
What a postal system we live with! Your letter is dated Sunday, postmarked Monday, and it arrives Thursday. The Pony Express did better than that.

September plans are still *en l'air* but France is not as much of an improbability as it seemed in March. Roger Straus has asked me to edit a volume of Colette's letters, which would mean an advance on or about September 15. *Alors* . . . On the other hand, I am contracted to teach through August 24 and possibly in the fall. I have been so drearily broke in the past six months that I shrink at running the risk again. But I'll know shortly what to do. If, for instance, FS&G wants the Jouhandeau anthology next fall, they might slip me a few more francs to visit him while he is still extant. The inscription on his most recent book said he was going blind. He'll be 89 in July.

Then, too, I may be in love again. As usual, with the wrong person, which means an only-too-familiar gamut of mute sulkings on my part. How this aspect of my—*mettons*—karma bores me. I want to be happy

(I mean requited of course) just once, for a weekend or two, and preferably in Paris.

Glenway's sister-in-law died a couple of weeks ago. Her husband woke up at 3 A.M. to find her rapidly cooling beside him. Lymphoma—I think that's the word; and mercifully without protracted pain. Now the agents of the Fisc and Parke-Bernet have arrived to catalogue all the Rothkos and Morandis and Monets and David Smiths (and two tiny R. Becks). Suddenly all the millions are blocked and money has to be borrowed from the bank to pay the cook. Perhaps we're lucky to have lived as the less fortunate live.

I saw *Quest* on the newsstand this week but was dashing to make a train so didn't get a copy. It looked prosperous. But why is Miss McKaughan behaving badly? Your piece should be run intact, especially the alphabetical parts . . .

No local news. My son telephoned the other evening to say that he and his wife are going to experiment with a 3 months' trial separation. Marriage licenses should be renewable annually, like dog or auto licenses.

Classes are winding up. In the next 10 days I must read dozens, or more exactly, hundreds of paragraphs, poems, storiettes, fragments, etc. from some 74 students. I'm tempted to give every 3rd student an A, and the rest B. I keep telling myself to heed Thoreau and "Simplify!" at any cost.

And I have a sty on my left lower eyelid. Psychosomatic, of course. Guilt vis-à-vis Roger Straus because that damned Colette scrapbook is still in the works. He bawled me out one day in February and the sty has been hovering ever since, even though we've hugged and made up long since. He wanted me to go with him to Paris last week but classes, love, poverty et al saved my day.

I'm reading *La Petite Dame*'s second volume on Gide. As dense and gossipy and absorbing as Boswell's Johnson. Did you see Gore Vidal in the *Times*? We must take care to outlive him.

June 26
Aspen

Ah, Robert, I missed you, but Freddie Laker is going to save us. Imagine New York to London—approximately London, that is—for $235! We must go this fall! I don't know how much longer I am going to be intact.

Just returned from Europe the day before yesterday. I was mostly in Chamonix, sleeping under huge granite boulders at the foot of the Dru while lightning clapped the top of it and thunder made the ground tremble. As for me, I was making notes. Do you remember the evening when you introduced the question of which novels had descriptions of weather in them? One more will have to be added to the list.

At the *douches municipales*, the woman who ran it asked me if I was English. When I said no, she confided that the English were the dirtiest people in the world "even the Arabs are cleaner." Were they like that at home, she wanted to know. What joy to say simply: worse. And in London, at Harrod's, they are selling Gerovital pills, the old age/anti-old age discovery of Dr. Ana Aslan of Bucharest. For £3.00 I would have a bit more confidence in them if there were a more recent photo of Dr. Aslan campaigning.

My daughters have all come home for the summer. One, the one from France, is staying with me (the house is very small) and already encouraging me to work harder and make the cabins above Carbondale inhabitable. She wants to go there and read and write (!) What can one write about at 19—I didn't say this, of course. She has some dreadful photos of me aged 14 and 16, given to her by her grandmother. Whoever that boy is, I don't like him.

I'm terribly sleepy by five in the afternoon and wake at three in the morning. I'm still in London. The hotel there was very small and pleasant, so long as you didn't have to bathe. It's just off Portobello Road in a section I was discovering for the first time (The Portobello Hotel, single about the size of your bathroom for £11–13 a night, not bad for London; very pleasant little restaurant downstairs). On the plane from London to Geneva I sat next to a Nigerian woman who'd been in Tokyo to a world health conference. Bureaucracy is the new upper class. She spoke a very pure university English . . .

What news of Jouhandeau? I've been looking everywhere for that story of his I so admire ("Cocu, Pendu . . . and something or other").

. . .

Salter mentions the Goncourts in his October 21 letter, a reference to a pair of brothers, Edmond and Jules de Goncourt. They were both writers; that is to say, they wrote together, collaborating on three novels, a book of nonfiction, and their journals. They published nothing individually and are thought to have never spent more than a day apart as adults.

. . .

October 21
Aspen

Gentlemen,
I've given up gin, I was beginning to look like Ford Maddox Ford. I've been working feverishly, on a desk made from some boards and two chairs set outside because the days have been so drowsy and mild and at night beneath a bright lamp on the dining room table, inspired by the fanaticism of Mishima. I'm nervous/writing things that depress me because they are not perfect, because they are wrong. I am waiting for the first glimpse, like that of a body beneath the water, pale, terrifying, that glimpse which says: it is there. Books opened, a few pages read and then cast aside litter every room, Turgenev, Hugo, Ford Maddox Ford, Babel, the Abbé de Brantôme. I can't find what I need, that's the only encouraging thing. I pulled down *All Quiet on the Western Front* a few nights ago. How thin it seemed. I've run out of money, haven't cut wood for the winter, my car sits outside with its engine half apart waiting for the mechanic to come back with a part—it's been waiting for a week, my finger is infected, I am very happy. Oh, how I would like to write this book!

I've been going through old notebooks. While doing it, I've been jotting down things to make up an index, mostly names, many of which I would never dream. I've also been listing cities, there's a lot about cities in them, occasional plots or ideas that seemed invulnerable at the time, and far too much, again and again, of one sexual affair. But I don't want to grind it up and use it all, I don't like journals. I like the Goncourts, but that was Paris. I've never read Léautaud's, perhaps in my more advanced old age. Can you believe that I miss you? I wish there were someone to scrawl at the bottom of this as George Sand's actress friend did at the bottom of her letter to Chopin: I, too, I, too, I, too.

. . .

The "Young" Phelps refers to in his October 26 letter is the eighteenth-century poet Edward Young, best known for his volume Night Thoughts. *Edmund Wilson was an influential American writer and literary critic.* Axel's Castle *and* To the Finland Station *are among his major works. Five volumes of his journals were published posthumously, as well as his correspondence with the writer Vladimir Nabokov.*

. . .

October 26
New York

Dear James-O,
I once dreamed of a story which would consist entirely of footnotes. The ur-text, the invisible story which all the footnote annotated, was the Genesis version of Adam and Eve, left implicit. There was no point to this method except that I love footnotes. Eliot's to "The Waste Land" have always seemed more interesting than the poem itself. I feel the same way about Marianne Moore's, and Auden's (in *The Double Man*) and even Empson's. When I was 12 I fell in love with S. S. Van Dine's detective stories because the bottom of the pages was twinkling with asterisks, obelisks, etc.

Curious that we should both be playing with journal orts these mid-autumn days. Last week I had a random 50 pages from my 1969 diaries Xeroxed and have since been trying to scissor and arrange them into—into what?—a shape of some sort. As for Léautaud, I promised months ago to select and translate some pages from his journal for *Paris Review*. I'll try to get at it, so you can see how sharp and tangy his personality is. He's more vulnerable than the Goncourts, who are essentially snipers. Léautaud is ruthless, but with himself as well as everyone else. And as precise and unsentimental about sex as any writer I've ever known.

"I am very happy." What an extraordinary claim. Bless you. I'm not sure I've ever heard anyone else say it. Try to determine exactly what particulars are involved. What odors. I tell myself "I am not unhappy." But I have a strickening sense of waste, of important days of my life slipping away without being marked, or used, or even abused. Do you know a couplet by Young:

"Like cats in air pumps, to subsist
we thrive
On joys too thin to keep the soul
alive."

But you are in love. I shouldn't quote such piffling witnesses in your presence.

I am reading Edmund Wilson's letters—brusque, bright, bullying and bookish, but joyously, un-academically so. He was not a man who could not remain alone in a room for weeks, providing he had books. And imagine teaching oneself Russian at 35, Hebrew at 60, Hungarian at 70! In his final months, he kept a sign taped on his oxygen tank at the foot of his bed, a sign in Hebrew, saying "Be strong, be strong!" It's not hard to love a man like that.

Your new life sounds bountiful—the reward of courage. But giving up gin is a grave matter. Are you sure you shouldn't reconsider? If I envy you anything more than having written *Sport*, it's not having yet cut your winter wood. How I'd love to be doing that for/with you! Cutting and piling wood has been, I think, the single most satisfying act of my entire life. Oak, birch, apple, ash, maple—and then their smoke on long, icy winter nights. Put your bed in front of the fireplace.

I'm trying to finish a story I began in 1958. It's called "In Praise of Billy Beaularis." My neurologist (a Swedish lady) is allowing me to resume the use of Dexedrine, so I'm modestly hopeful.

1978–1980
Over and Out

As early as 1970, Phelps mentioned difficulty writing legibly and added, "The fact is, it gets harder and harder for me even to type legibly." Whether this was to blame for his infrequent letters to Salter is hard to say. In any case, he wrote only once each in 1978 and 1980, perhaps due in part to a full slate of teaching duties at Manhattanville and the New School. He also talked of meeting the actress Jeanne Moreau, who wanted to film Colette's novel Chéri, *as well as her* La Naissance du Jour. *Salter, meanwhile, saw* Solo Faces *published. His travels, at least those recorded in the letters from those years, took him to Bora-Bora and Tahiti.*

1978

February 25
Aspen

Robert, nonpareil—
There's a piece of mine in the current *Quest*. I'd be very eager to have your reaction to it, does it interest you to read it, because it's the same subject though not of course the same style as the book. I'm just finishing, may even finish today at about six in the evening if my nerves can be calmed; they're jumping like fleas.

My God, how I have worked this year! I began with the outline on July 10th, the actual writing on August 1st and with few exceptions have been at it every day since.

Karyl Roosevelt arrived here yesterday with her young companion (Ted Bent?) and we're supposed to have dinner tonight. Lorenzo wants me to arrange for her to come to Tahiti to comfort him in the spring, my first real pimping. I'm looking forward to it. Do drop me a brief line.

March 5
Aspen

We are always talking about you, especially when Karyl Roosevelt is here. Sometimes Peggy Clifford and I talk about you, sometimes I read through your book which is simply my single favorite book, my best-loved book and most mysterious—no matter how often I read it, it seems there are things I've never seen before, which appeared between readings.

You mentioned having English edition copies of it in back and offered to send some. I can't remember why I said I'd pick them up but now I find I cannot live without them. Will you mail them to me? At least two or three more if you like. People are always wanting to borrow or read my copy and occasionally there is somebody worthy of being given one to keep.

I mailed *Solo Faces* off to Little, Brown on Friday. I am serene, nervous, constantly reviewing portions of it in my mind and finding them imperfect. But then, everything in it is so appallingly familiar to me. RSVP.

March 9

Dear Jim,
The sight of your envelope in the mailbox left me blanched with guilt—your last letter and your lambent descant on mt.-climbing still unacknowledged!—and I hurtled up the stairs and turned on the typewriter this instant.

Of course you shall have copies of *The Lit. Life* as soon as I can get them wrapped and to the P.O.

"Man Is His Own Star" is a very elegant piece of work, at once tender and austere, and conveying the mystique of men and mountains with intimacy and authority. I have read it three times, and its pace and composition are very professional. And the final paragraph—the nipper—is like ending on B flat in alt—perfect intonation and not a quaver. Solo Faces itself can't be better, only more so. When is publication skedded?

The past few weeks have been stupefyingly jammed. Besides teaching at Manhattanville and the New School, I have been trying to finish a story begun before Christmas; reading proofs and working with the designer of *Belles Saisons* (the Colette picture album); trying to write a 6,000-word article on 5th Avenue; failing to write a decent review of a friend's novel. And now Carson McCullers's sister Rita Smith has suddenly collapsed with something as yet undiagnosed and I have been asked to take over her story-writing workshop and can't think of how to say no. And earlier this week I had lunch with Jeanne Moreau who plans to film both *Chéri* and *La Naissance du Jour* and asked me to help with the scripts. And too many people have been spending the night here—not romantically, for God's sake, but simply to save hotel bills—and I am supposed to write a memoir of Louise Bogan for her biographer; and I want to see O'Horgan's version of *The Tempest* and even more, I want to get out of half a dozen imminent dinners.

Hug Karyl Roosevelt for me. I think I last beheld her in a local post office and promised myself to take her to lunch at 1 Fifth, and then—what?—Becki must have gotten pneumonia, or my granddaughter arrived, or I visited Glenway in New Jersey and was glamorously clawed by one of his niece's pet Siberian tigers (each weighs 200 pounds at age 8 months and they come at you—playfully—with the impact of half the Princeton football team.)

I've turned the page and can't remember where I was. So I'll try to round up some *Lit Lives* (sic) and get this stamped and on its way.

Much love to all your household.

. . .

Robert Bolt was a screenwriter who wrote the scripts for Lawrence of Arabia, A Man for All Seasons, *and* Doctor Zhivago. *David Lean directed both* Lawrence of Arabia *and* Doctor Zhivago.

. . .

March 28
Aspen

Dear Robert,

You are bathing in glory—Jeanne Moreau and films of *La Naissance du Jour*, lunches, theatre, dinners with the titans of art. Life in exile is bitter in comparison. Here there are nothing but real estate and the Kennedys. Occasionally someone leaving town will drop off their groceries rather than throwing them out. In consequence I've a lot of cheese, mayonnaise, and countless bottles of salad dressing. The refrigerator looks like City Market.

I'm at rest and nervous as a cat. I swore to read *Anna Karenina* but haven't had the composure to even sit down in the sun for a few hours. The winter is over. The snow vanished in a week. Bob Ginna says he loves my book and then I've heard nothing further for three weeks. It will be published next spring. I have very grave doubts about it even as an entertainment. Certainly I've never been able to entertain anyone before and I'm very tired of writing about people without education, intelligence or ideas. I'd like you to read it before I sit down to rewrite, but I know you can't do it now. It's not very long though. There's no one here to read it or read to. I'm bored with auto-discourse.

Karyl Roosevelt is long gone. Don't forget to hug her for me. Don't forget to send *The Literary Lifes*. My friend Lorenzo Semple had his 55th birthday two days ago, he insisted it was his 45th. I gave him a copy of the new Samuel Johnson biography and on the card wrote some moving lines about Johnson from the flyleaf, addressing them to Lorenzo. He was so drunk he tore the jacket off the book with the wrapping paper and the wittiness of allowing him to find the very same lines on the flyleaf was thus blunted. Instead I was astonished to see him almost burst into tears, deeply touched, while I tried to explain I hadn't written them. No, no, he insisted, as if I were always too modest. Finally I gave up. He lives the life of a pasha. He's going to Bora Bora for the making of his movie, a remake of *Hurricane* by Dino de Laurentiis. But they don't have a leading lady. The movie's due to begin shooting in four weeks and will take five months (!) to make. Robert Bolt is down in Tahiti with David Lean. They're engaged in some long and worthy project. Lorenzo had dinner with Bolt who, discussing screenwriting, advised him, "My boy! The money! Never take your eye from it for a second."

Write when you can. I embrace.

April 5
Aspen

Dear Robt,

Oh yes, Asolo. I was in Venice in October about three years ago. The walks through its streets, the empty Lido, the green air, not to mention the boat to Torcello and lunch there at—I forget the name—the small hotel. I never visited Diagelev's grave, or Rolfe's or, now, Stravinsky's. I never had dinner at Harry's Bar though I had a martini there one evening, icy cold in a glass that was colder yet. And Verona is not far off, and Ravenna and Bologna. I want to breathe a foreign air and imagine a foreign life. I want to learn new words: that is one of the most thrilling things on earth.

Here is the book. You know its unworthy genesis, but forget that. Little, Brown likes it very much. They've made only minor suggestions and want to publish it this coming February. I should have it back to them by mid-May at the latest. I gave it to them sooner than I would have ordinarily and there are many things I'm dissatisfied with, there are things on every page. I tried to write a book that people would like to read, would like very much to read, an adventure, there was no other purpose. Of course, there are certain standards one hates to abandon, but first I wrote, on the inside cover of my notebook: No Fine Writing! So with these modest but for me novel aims, I offer it to you. Judge it by its peers. Be as harsh as you like, I will love you no less. I would just like your impressions and reactions and the level of your pleasure or displeasure.

I'm so tired of writing about people who have no intellectual existence. Perhaps that's all I know. I've finally started *Anna Karenina*. I did see an episode of it on television while in Phoenix (I also saw *The Barretts of Wimpole Street*, what a lame, old, foolish trotter) but found it unsatisfying. I thought Anna and Vronsky and Oblonsky were all wrong and there was a haste and brittleness that bothered me.

My two oldest daughters are in London. I've begun to get some very good letters from them, letters that reveal them in ways I never suspected or had given up hoping for. We had dinner the other night with a large family that was in Aspen together, gathered from all over for a vacation and reunion. The mother, a Philadelphia Grace, her two sons and daughter, all in their thirties, two stepsons, and the ex-wife of another stepson and all the attendant wives, husbands and children. At dinner there were only the major figures and their good nature, good manners and great sense of well-being and fun was, for me, a revelation. They were not that brilliant or clever, but they did get along with one another marvelously well. The mother told me I was the funniest man she'd ever met though I don't recall saying anything humorous to her. I'm told my face is very transparent.

I want to travel. I want to be an elegant older man that people believe may still achieve something. I want to see Duse's grave.

Well, I miss you as you can see.

. . .

Franca Tasso worked with Salter on the film he directed, 1969's Three.

. . .

May 24
Aspen

Dearest Robt,
I sailed for a long time on the news you gave me when I called. In fact I'm still going. The book for $22, that says something. I don't think I'll ever win a prize but I'll always be grateful to Glenway. I've only seen him twice in my life. The first time, in your little office, he told about the death of his father and bathing the old man and holding him in

his arms. There was one other occasion though when he seemed very present: that was at the Russian Tea Room one day when we were having lunch, I think it was your birthday, you were probably in your thirties it was so long ago, and you said something he'd said, that literature was made up of uninventable lines. Oh, the patience to collect and know them!

An Italian lady, very nice, sent me a magazine with an article on Asolo. Ravishing. It's been on the map, so to speak, since the exile there of Caterina Cornaro, the queen of Cyprus (!) in 1489. Perhaps I'll be there for the 500th anniversary, I'd love it. Robert Browning lavished affection on it, and so did his son whose villa has been made into a hotel. The English have always liked the town and gone there. In fact it was an Englishwoman, Lyndall Birch, who first told me about it.

I'm thinking of Franca Tasso who sent me the article. She's witty, hardworking and lonely. She lived for four or five years with some set designer and then left him abruptly when she discovered he had never broken off a prior relationship with a secretary. These demands for sexual exclusivity. Of course, they are not only made by women, but they are the most maddening thing on earth. I'm reading *Portrait of a Marriage*. I remember when Becki said it was the best book of the year—we were having dinner at Yvonne's, gigot and flageolets and wonderful stories about Robert Motherwell and romantic dreams. Anyway, I like the book very much. Vita sounds so much like Ford Maddox Ford, *The Good Soldier*, in her sections, that quintessential Englishness.

I mailed off the revised *Solo Faces* two days ago. Endless fretting and worrying about things that are at their best imperfect anyway. I added a chapter, changed the ending, and did innumerable small things throughout. It's a bit better. It's astonishing how the crossing out of a line, sometimes a phrase, or the substitution of something right for something false can suddenly let light in on an entire chapter. My typist accidentally left out seven lines at the end of Chapter 16 and I said, wonderful, it's much better without them. I'm already ashamed of the first version. Can you just throw it in an envelope and send it back to me? I promise you the first and freshest copy of the book itself in return. Ginna has gone off to Dublin & England for a five week holiday so I won't know anything further until he returns but I think publication will be next February or March. I plan to come east in July, probably mid-July, for about ten days to see my mother and attend to whatever. We're going to sign, you and I, a pact in blood: Europe. Please, news.

. . .

James Jones was the author of From Here to Eternity *and* The Thin Red Line, *among other works. He served in the Pacific and was most acclaimed for his writing on World War II.*

. . .

July 18
Bora Bora

Soon to walk along the beach for a mile or so for a drink and dinner.

My plea for a look at the ocean was answered—Lorenzo sent tickets, Aspen–Bora Bora. They're shooting his movie *The Hurricane* here. The behavior of the actors, as usual, is detestable. As to their performances, various opinions.

We are in a little house with a tin roof, no electricity, little water and much happiness. There are no screens. The mosquitoes are descendants of those James Jones once knew. We're moving into a tent that has netting. It's ten feet from the sea.

Very expensive here. New York a bargain in comparison. I haven't written a word in weeks.

. . .

The actor Trevor Howard appeared in a number of notable films, among them The Third Man *and* Gandhi.

. . .

August 2
Leaving Tahiti

I will never forget three things: the rain, sleeping in a tent for two weeks, and Trevor Howard's nose.

In the middle of the greatest ocean, we ate nothing but pasta, veal, and steak prepared by Italian chefs, and clattered around in a war-surplus jeep from Vietnam. As Gauguin wrote, after days of sailing they came to a small island, almost nothing on it. Three inhabitants: one was the governor, the second a *huissier*, and the third *un marchand de tabac* who sold postage stamps. Already.

Here one understands Algeria, Indochina, and for that matter, S. Africa. As much as I detest politics, I detest colonials more.

August 7
Chilmark, MA

Dear Jim,

This can't compare with Bora-Bora, but there is a century-old lighthouse and for the first time in my life I've become intimate with the sea. It's a soap opera: something eventful going on every hour: terns, tides, gulls, clouds—all busy and watchable. I'm up at dawn and in bed by 8; see almost no one; and love it. You sound marvelous. When is the book skedded? We're here until 9/15.

. . .

Rust Hills was the fiction editor for Esquire *for many years. James Norman Hall was the author of* Mutiny on the Bounty, *among other titles.* Daniel Martin *was a novel by John Fowles.*

. . .

August 11
Aspen

Dear Robt,

It now seems a dream, very distant and unrecoverable, something like the opening chapter of *Tales of the South Pacific*. We spent the last two nights in a fabulous house on top of a mountain in Tahiti, the house of James Norman Hall's daughter and her idiot husband, that is to say boring. They weren't there. They have small parts in the movie and were in Bora Bora living on their cabin cruiser at $600 each a week salary. There was a Frenchwoman who was a kind of guest & caretaker. Marvelous exhausted face and those beautiful French legs. She'd been born in Algeria. I liked her. She was very candid, she thought I could speak French, I seem to remember because I used the word *diminutif*. The first night we stumbled down the vast lawns in the dark trying to find Hall's grave. She couldn't seem to remember where it was. Finally we located it behind some chicken wire and beneath some dead leaves, the only thing on the entire estate that wasn't perfectly looked after.

I read a hundred pages of *Daniel Martin* while I was on Bora Bora, found it uninteresting. Finally retreated into a biography of Cavafy that I'd brought along, not a very carefully done book but nonetheless fascinating. Furthermore—I don't know how to explain this—I believe the book, not merely because it's true, while I didn't believe the others. My own book is back from the copy editor & I must go through it and return it to them by about the 20th. There are a couple of serious possibilities for its being excerpted, one *Sports Illustrated*—don't laugh—and the other *Esquire*. I had a very nice note from Rust Hills. *The Paris Review* wants to take the d'Annunzio piece which *Quest* paid me for but finally decided they couldn't use; I'm going to rewrite it for them. I'm also trying to write a story for their 25th anniversary issue.

I don't suppose you have a telephone up there?

Europe, I'm still thinking of Europe. I long to see you.

1979

. . .

Ben Sonnenberg was the founder and publisher of Grand Street.

. . .

January 12
Aspen

Dear Robert,
That review in *Time* was foolish and uncalled-for. The book is wonderful. Ben Sonnenberg wrote to me about it the other day.

The best season for work is here. The snow is so high it has almost covered the fence around the house. I'm reading the early Powell novels. The thing I like most about them is their assumption of an intelligent reader. There are occasional pieces of dialogue, completely unexpected and unprepared-for, that are like slaps in the face. I was working on a story called "Twenty Minutes" about a woman riding up in the hills who is thrown from her horse and badly hurt, but the woman who had the important details some of which I got from her one evening, has moved to Santa Fe. What can this mean except that I was meant to work on something else? I had a play sketched out called *Honor*—not a very good title but it described what it was about—and just came across a description in French in *Venusberg* of a play by Galsworthy called *Loyalties* that more or less is about the same thing. One of the joys of living here is that there's no chance in the world that the library will have any such work.

The early readings of my book seem to be encouraging. Of course, it hasn't hit the esteemed NY critics yet. Irwin Shaw sent a very nice puff. And very promptly I said, but Irwin Shaw . . . ? and was silenced with, Nonsense, Shaw's is a money quote, far more important than James Dickey or any of those people. The jacket—did I say this—is handsome, the best jacket I've ever had. Of course, it's no *Belles Saisons*, but then, I'm not with Farrar Straus.

We were talking about a minor writer last night whose promiscuous daughter was named Rhianin, it means something very fancy in Welsh, someone said. "Loved by druids, or something," she remembered. "More like 'loved by myriads,'" her husband remarked.

I didn't send you bound galleys—I've rewritten a lot and done a new ending—but you shall have a first copy. No plans for the summer yet.

July 20
New York

Fratello mio,

I dash to the typewriter to acknowledge arrival of the book and letter—a little anxiously, since the letter is dated July 7th, which means that on top of everything else, you may have been uneasy about seeming silence on my part. Peter Deane happens to be here this week, and our respective copies arrived hand in hand a few minutes ago. A little later in the day, I shall sit down with my martini and read—or reread—the entire text. Then I'll write again, less incoherently.

Meantime I missed the Prescott review, but I'll hunt it down. I can't imagine what he could have said that hurt you. Have you had any word about the Sunday *Times*? I don't think I've missed an issue since May, but I was on Martha's Vineyard over the 4th and may not have seen that week's book section. Does Little, Brown subscribe to a clipping service? Peter told me Robt. Manning's wife reviewed it beautifully in one of the Boston papers.

I wish you could be here—both of you—for a couple of hours so I could make you proper martinis and hug you both. I ache at the thought of your "melancholy." Fuck Peter Prescott. You know and Kay knows and I know and Peter Deane and any number of others know that you are, everywhere, an exquisite, gallant maker of English language sentences. (Oh, by the way, *The Paris Review* with your marvelous D'Annunzio chronicle came yesterday. I love it—the form even more than the elegantly selective contents: it's your form: the alphabet. You must write your next novel in the form of an alphabet. Yes.)

Suddenly I can't bear the thought that you're miserable. I'm going to try to reach you by phone. It's 10:45 A.M. here, so you should be awake out in Aspen. *Verrons . . .*

You were,—awake, that is. It was wonderful to hear your voices. As soon as I get to MV, I'll start plotting to get to Sag Harbor. Meantime much love to you both.

À bientôt,

Robert

(Imagine Mike Dirda having reviewed your book! He was here in May and we talked about you extensively but he has not mentioned having written about you. He's very bright, and barely 30! Ach!)

August 28
Sag Harbor

Dear Robert,
Slow, steady rain, so beautiful in Paris, so terrible here in the woods. The postage stamps are stuck together. So are your legs when you sleep.

A huge fin was seen on Sunday cruising parallel to the beach, about two hundred feet out. And a record mako shark, I hear, was caught off Montauk. Sumo doesn't go in the water, so he doesn't care, and Joe Fox assures me there is no record of a human shark-bite injury in Eastern Long Island. I, myself, go in at every chance. The other night, drunk and naked, we waded out into the crashing waves at two in the morning. The sea this year is warmer than I can ever remember.

Karyl's out here until the end of the summer now. She's going to talk to you about your cat. You are saving a beautiful creature from destruction and all cats, two and four-legged, will be grateful.

Wouldn't it be fine to be able to write a story in an afternoon, the way these literary swashbucklers did in their youth? I've been working for weeks on one and I still hate it. To prove it can be done I occasionally open Chekov and then close it in anger. He has ruined it for the rest of us.

Here's the Bourjaily review. I'm trying to have *Solo Faces* bought by Penguin. Peter Matthiessen's son (!) there likes it very much.

Kelley won't take dogs. Can you ask a motel or two?

. . .

The letter Salter mentions was to Roger Straus of Farrar, Straus and Giroux. In it, Salter asked him to publish A Sport and a Pastime *as a trade paperback.*

. . .

September 5
Sag Harbor

Dear Robert,
I wrote to Roger. You were right, it did no harm. He called to say the letter made sense and he would reconsider. He asked for a copy of the book which I'll send as soon as I get home.

We're staying this ultimate week in Joe Fox's house which is right on Sag Pond and within sight of the sea. Rabbits wander onto the lawn to the inexpressible delight of Sumo. There's a canoe to go to the beach.

I read Roth's new book yesterday. He has one sure talent: he writes one story extremely well, the story of himself and Newark told again and again, always achingly candid, remorseless, cruel. He reminds me of Woody Allen, an Allen who knows something. These guys are suffocating me. Karyl wants to get you a cat. Call her.

October 3
Aspen?

Cher Maître,
Everyone has seen your book [*Belles Saisons*], I showed them only enough to kindle their appetites and desires. I read it through with the utmost joy. It is a lovely book. Dennis Howard, stranded actor, who works in the (best) bookstore here, was ravished by it. He's ordering a dozen to start. How I would have liked to have lived in France in the

'20s and '30s. That was my true period and place, with occasional trips to New York. Life has been good but I would like to drink it again.

I'm still at work, disheartened, on the final chapter of my book [*Solo Faces*]. I've rewritten it twice since New York. It still eludes me somehow. I know just what it should be but haven't been able to do it. This morning was cold. The sunlight shooting from the leaves, sky clear, fall in the air. In a few minutes I'm going to try again, somewhere in all that boring clay is the shape I'm looking for.

Dinner the night before last with the owner of Uriah Heep, a boutique here. She's a manic woman with hair as shiny black as a piano. Also a marvelous cook. She told about an obscene phone call. It was last Christmas. She'd been mailing packages all week and on Sunday the phone rang. Hello, she said. A man's voice said, how'd you like to get your box off this afternoon? I didn't know you were open today! she cried. Dismayed silence. The poor man hung up.

A farmhouse between Florence and Sienna is available from the owners who're coming to dinner this Saturday. I miss that room, those books, old Maugham.

. . .

The American journalist Alma Reed fell in love with Felipe Carrillo Puerto, governor of the Yucatan, while working there during the 1920s, not the 1930s, as Salter has it.

. . .

October 21
Aspen

Robert, my best,
Yr letter sounded a little discouraged. Your new cat will set you on your feet. There's nothing like a little new pussy as the gallants at the Jerome assure. It's almost snowing here. There is that dampness and uneasy warmth in the air. A big storm is predicted for tonight, very bad for the elk as the season on them has just opened and on dry ground they can hear the crackling of the leaves for a mile and move serenely away.

I'm awaiting the galleys. They'll be here in three weeks or so. With the scratchy beginnings from your (Peter's) little bureau I managed to devise a new ending. I forgot to send you the so-called review from *City News*. I think she's trying to write a good one but hardly knows how. Probably she's one of those visual people.

There was some thought of coming east, mainly to try and arrange Martha's Vineyard for the spring, but now I don't know if I'll be able to. If I am it will be in mid-November. I'd love it. Probably won't happen.

Kay sold a piece to *Cosmopolitan*. The last couple of days we were in Bora Bora she began to scurry around and get information about the various shacks for rent and the hotels, the same on Tahiti as we were leaving. Translating it all into go-go language she wrote a travel article and they just sent her a check. I'm promised a wonderful dinner (bought, not cooked) but unfortunately the classic restaurants are closed at the moment. Now she's working on a script—the one I was doing some research on in NY. It's about the love affair between Alma Reed and the ill-fated Puerto Carrillo, governor of the Yucatan in the '30s. She'll probably sell it for a bundle. One of the possible producers was here a few days ago. He told her he was here with a four month old baby but her hearing isn't very good and she asked him when they met where the "formidable" baby was. They all are.

Ah, the sun has come out. To work.

October 31
Aspen

Dear Robt,
1500 tickets have been sold (at $6 per) to the Halloween Ball tonight at the Hotel Jerome—this in a town of 6,000 people. It's the big event of the year. Lorenzo is burning holes in an old Brooks Bros. pin-stripe suit, cutting off a leg of the pants and otherwise shredding it—he's going as the US dollar.

I finished the last page and the last delicious word of your book over the weekend and mailed it back to you to be inscribed. Them I'm going to put it away and get another copy to reread and let people paw over.

Unusually mild fall. I cut the last of the firewood this morning, a great dead standing fir tree not too far from the road, about ten miles from here up Independence Pass. Wish you'd been with me. My dog was sitting in the middle of a snowy road—not a single car but mine—watching me struggle with the big logs. He's sleeping beneath the bed at the moment. Do you have your cat?

1980

. . .

Donald Sutherland is an actor known for his work in films such as The Dirty Dozen *and* MASH. *The actor Rex Harrison earned an Academy Award for his work in the film* My Fair Lady. *He also appeared in films such as* Cleopatra *and* The Agony and the Ecstasy. *Rachel Roberts, who had been married to Rex Harrison, was an actress who appeared in two major films of the British New Wave,* Saturday Night and Sunday Morning *and* This Sporting Life.

. . .

March 5
Aspen

Dear Robert,
Fayette Hickox (?) was interviewing for a job at *Life*. *The Paris Review* is really a springboard. At dinner in Little Italy Donald Sutherland told me that Rachel Roberts had drunk a bottle of lye the night her ex-husband, whom she thought she had won back but hadn't, opened in a revival of *My Fair Lady* in Los Angeles. Sutherland also told the following about Rex Harrison, with whom he had appeared in a small role in Donald's first play. He saw Harrison some years later at a party. "You don't remember me, do you?" he said. Harrison looked up from his plate. "No," he said.

"I appeared with you in ________," Donald said. "Can't you see I'm eating dinner?" Harrison said. The charm of the rich.

. . .

Phelps mentions Natalia Danesi Murray and her great consort Janet Flanner. Ms. Murray published Flanner's letters to her as Darlinghissima: Letters to a Friend. *Further reflections on the pair can be found in William Murray's book,* Janet, My Mother, and Me: A Memoir of Growing up with Janet Flanner and Natalia Danesi Murray.

. . .

June 7
New York

Dear James,
I seem to remember a blue mailbox along Lobsterville Road called Pfluger, or Phluger. We'll be able to flash mirror-messages as drinky time approaches. Becki's house is on the water, off a rutted creek bed I call Tobacco Toad, which runs parallel to Lobsterville Road. The sunsets in August can be abashing.

Happy birthday. I'll mix an especially potent martini the afternoon of the 10th, and toast your coming east. Tell Kay to hug you for me.

I used to see Natalia Danesi Murray quite often, when her great consort Janet Flanner was among us. I wish she'd write her memoirs, or persuade her son to do them for her. I saw her in April, at Glenway's 79th birthday party and she looked great.

There is a shorter and better life of Wagner than [Ernest] Newman's. *Richard Wagner, The Man, His Mind, and His Music*, by Robert Gutman. It's in paperback; Knopf's, I think.

I thought your West Point piece very professional, very trim and lively. Naturally I wanted it to be a memoir of J. Salter. But I enjoyed it as it was. The day it came out I met Karyl Roosevelt and we both agreed to write you about it. But instead I read it to my Journalism workshop that evening and never got around to the letter.

The North Point Press sounds providential, especially "their ambition to keep their list in print." With most publishers these days, remaindering is part of publication. Thank you for sending them *The Lit Life*. Should I perhaps write Mr. Shoemaker?

It's Saturday morning and the "sky is darkening like a stain." I'm standing at my fifth floor window and the curtains are beginning to flap. I'm hoping for a good storm. Over and out.

Robert

. . .

Phelps and Salter did exchange letters after 1980, though there was no regularity to the exchange. Salter traveled extensively after 1980. Phelps continued working much in the same manner he had had throughout his career. It was during these years that his health began to deteriorate. His Parkinson's disease was still more pronounced. The completion of his final books must have been a feat. Parkinson's disease, however, is not generally considered fatal. Other problems arose, and he was diagnosed with colon cancer. No letters from Phelps to Salter exist from this period. Salter's contain no mention of the illnesses plaguing Phelps. They seem instead intended to lift his spirits, for they are sprinkled liberally with details of travel and gossip. Salter recounts seeing him for the last time when Phelps was "lying beneath a single white sheet in the heat of July. Very ill. He could no longer speak. He held my hand for a long time and gave me what I can only think of as canny glances." Phelps died of colon cancer in 1989. Below is the note Salter sent to Phelps's wife, the painter Rosemarie Beck, upon learning of his death:

. . .

August 3

I wept when I read the obituary. I want to write to you but I can't, it's too painful. I'll do it later.

I loved Robert. I love him still and always. He was an anchor to seaward for me and one of the few pure voices of my life.

Next weekend, August 10–11, I expect to be in the city. Let's have dinner Saturday night. I'll talk to you before then.

I admire you so.

Jim

. . . .

Index

D